Abused
By
The Church

From Victim To Victor
How To Overcome Spiritual Abuse

Donna Rigney

Table of Contents

Dedication

This book is dedicated to my wonderful husband, my understanding family and faithful friends: Thank you Jack, for all your encouragement and continuous support. To each and every one of my children: Thank you for allowing me the time and freedom to spend so many hours working on this book. Your consideration made it so much easier for me. A special thank you to all my friends and church family who cheered me on to complete this project: Your prayers were answered.

I extend a sincere word of thanks to all those who sacrificially shared their stories with me. Your experiences inspired and motivated me to write this book. Undoubtedly, your faithfulness to the Lord amidst the storms of abuse will serve as an inspiration to all who read this work.

Introduction

One quiet afternoon, a knock at our front door transformed our peaceful existence into a sudden burst of activity. My husband and I had retired and moved to a vacation resort in central Florida. Leisurely traveling in our new diesel pusher motor home had become our way of life. For the first year of retirement, we just kicked back, spent time with family and friends, and toured the United States enjoying the beauty of our country. Settling in rural Florida had not been our plan—but it happened.

The friendly vacation community we came upon during our travels seemed to call out to us to stay. Unable to resist that internal summons, we settled there. Living amongst people who came from all over the USA and Canada proved to be enjoyable and very insightful.

Getting back to the knock at our door: A wonderful gentleman I had met briefly at the pool stood on our back step and asked me if I could do him a favor. He oversaw the church service that was held Sunday mornings for those visiting and residing at the resort. He explained that the pastor who had been faithfully serving the community was no longer able to conduct the service. Sheepishly, he asked if I could help him out and preach in two weeks on Mother's Day.

And so began a new era in our lives. That one Sunday service marked the transition from retirees to pastors of the 'church in the lodge.' Our congregation was unlike any we had ever served in the past. This community changed continuously. A few members lived permanently in the resort, but most traveled there on vacation. Some stayed for a few days, while others resided there for the winter months.

This unique congregation afforded my husband and me a wonderful opportunity to minister to people from almost every state in the USA and from different districts in Canada. As we prayed together, enjoyed pot luck cook-outs, or went on motorcycle rides with one another our friendships and communications deepened.

Many of these wonderful people began to share their very traumatic experiences with us. To our utter dismay, stories of abuse within the church community became commonplace. Hearing these incidences of abuse pierced our hearts and began to lay the foundation for our ministry to bring healing to the victims of spiritual abuse. Week after week sincere, gentle-hearted people related their painful accounts of abuse within the walls of the church. Many still suffering from the effects of their mistreatment, explained how they had been victimized by controlling leaders. Others were heart-broken from being deceived by leaders they had trusted and depended on. Worse still was the pain of those who related personal stories of the sexual misconduct of their ministers and the demoralizing effect it had on their lives.

Sadly to say, stories of kind-hearted people being taken for granted and used by ambitious ministers became routine. These wounded individuals related that once they gave wholeheartedly of their financial support or in many cases their physical labor, they were discarded. Individuals who had been pillars in their churches were now no longer attending any church. Fearful, disappointed and very disillusioned, they could not be convinced to reconnect with the body of Christ.

As time progressed in our transitional community, some courageously let down their walls of suspicion and began attending church. Despite the fact that there were those who had suffered life changing abuse, they found the safety and security that the body of Christ offered comforting and healing.

During the ensuing years in Central Florida, many new relationships were established and other tragic stories emerged. Not only were we listening to congregants divulge their accounts of mistreatment at the hands of their leaders, but now accounts were being related to us of the abusive treatment of humble ministers by some of their congregants. Equally as shocking and just as abusive, were the actions perpetrated against God's lowly servants. These men and women were targeted with false accusations, neglect, rejection, prejudice and ingratitude. Slander and malicious gossip destroyed some of their churches. Discouraged and deeply heartbroken a few pastors left the ministry forever.

The Great Escape

These abusive situations have caused a tidal wave of bitterness and suspicion to engulf the church. Various sects and their leaders are held under a magnifying glass of intensive scrutiny. Because of this, individuals and their families are staying home from church, opting to pray together in a safe zone rather than take the chance of encountering an abusive pastor or controlling leader.

Their fears, though often grounded in fact, are perpetuating an atmosphere of segregation. The rich treasures that the body of Christ has to offer are being withheld from them. With no one to lead, correct or instruct these individuals, they are easily deceived. Frequently, difficulties arise in their lives when they need the helping hand of a brother or sister, and there is no one there to comfort or support them. This is not God's plan, but it is happening anyway.

Walking alone through life is not the way to happiness and freedom. Walking with our hand in His and in our brother's will empower us and provide the necessary support we all need to fulfill our God given assignments.

God the Father established the Church through His Son and declared that *".the gates of Hades will not overcome it" (Matthew 16: 18)*. It appears that the enemy is attempting to do just that—prevail against the Church and overcome it. Thank God, He has the final word on that matter; Satan won't defeat His church.

Trumpeting the Cause of the Defenseless

The Lord is determined to rescue His bride. *"Speak up for those who cannot speak for themselves, for the rights of all who are destitute. Speak up and judge fairly; defend the rights of the poor and needy" (Proverbs 31: 8-9.)* In order for the victims of abuse to be equipped to recover, they must be given a voice. For too long, perpetrators of abuse have instilled fear and shame in their victims. Frequently, threats of retaliation and other forms of intimidation have crippled many into silence. This is especially true of abuse that has been suffered through the actions of the clergy. A veil of secrecy and shame has enabled this abuse to continue unabated.

Jesus told those who believed in Him, *"Then you will know the truth, and the truth will set you free'" (John 8:32)*. If just knowing the truth sets people free; then, how much more will speaking the truth in love release those held in bondage to past abuse. Those things hidden in darkness don't diminish in size or influence. Quite the contrary, they grow and eventually dominate victims' lives. The damage can be catastrophic. Depressions, anxiety, distrusting those in authority, fear of attending church, segregation from others, and suspicion: are but a few of the effects of this kind of trauma.

Authentic examples of mistreatment will be presented throughout this work in order to give a voice to those held in the grip of silence. The improper attitudes, actions and expectations of both leaders and congregants will be exposed. Because simply stating the problem and not offering a workable solution won't accomplish a true work of restoration, mindsets that foster an atmosphere that can often trigger and allow abuse will be elaborated on. Also, Biblical guidelines will be set forth to help empower people to recognize and leave abusive situations without bitterness or regret.

These instructions, grounded in Scripture, will act as a means of rescue for those who have been silenced and left in the dark—stranded and desperate. The victims of abuse can then begin the work of reconstructing their emotional and spiritual lives. Powerful Scriptural truths will initiate healing and help those isolated from other believers to fearlessly reconnect with a healthy church.

A Helping Hand Extended To Restore His People

Many future leaders are currently sitting on the sidelines watching others serve in His kingdom. The call has been given to His angels to bring them forth and plant them where they will be fruitful and fulfilled. These desperate hurting individuals are the very ones He will fill with His Spirit and use to gather in the great harvest. Souls must be saved. Jesus established His church for this purpose. He will not rest until His dejected, wounded ones are delivered and restored to their position in His end time army.

Along with those victimized by abusive leaders and their concerned loved ones, those who have lost their way as leaders will be extended a helping hand as well. *"My brothers, if one of you should wander from the truth and someone should bring him back, remember this: Whoever turns a sinner from the error of his way will save him from death and cover over a multitude of sins" (James 5:19-20).* Most leaders begin their ministry with pure motives and strong convictions. After years of faithful service, some have fallen prey to the snares of the enemy. Carrots of pride and selfish ambition have been dangled in front of them by the enemy. Deceived by the enticement of riches and power, many well meaning leaders have embraced carnal pleasure and relinquished their calling. *"For where you have envy and selfish ambition, there you will find disorder and every evil practice" (James 3:16).*

Tragically, there are many ministers who have been victimized by the actions of unappreciative or abusive congregants. Scandalized by their mistreatment, vast multitudes have given up and join the ranks of those who sit on the sidelines of His kingdom and simply watch as others accomplish those things that they dreamed of doing. Despair, cloaked in apathy, imprisons them. The hour is at hand for them to be delivered out of failure and placed back at the head of His army. No longer will fear of man hinder them. Instead, God will use them to strike fear in the heart of the enemy. The Lord is longing for the restoration of those chosen to serve in His kingdom: *"The harvest is plentiful but the workers are few. Ask the Lord of the harvest, therefore, to send out workers into his harvest field" (Matthew 9: 37-38).*

Exposing the Truth in Love

The terrible problem of abuse within the walls of the church, both by the leaders towards the people and that committed against the leaders by their congregants, has to be addressed and honestly dealt with for the Lord to be glorified in His church. In order for Him to be truly glorified, love and forgiveness must prevail. *"A new command I give you: Love one another. As I have loved you, so you must love one another. By this all men will know that you are my disciples, if you love one another" (John 13:34-35).*

To accomplish this, *Abused by the Church* will present many factual reports of people who were mistreated by the leaders in their churches. The names and places of those involved in each situation have been changed to protect the privacy of all—both leaders and congregants. The purpose of this book is not to bring accusations, nor to slander any, but to bring reform, deliverance and reconciliation.

Seeing and understanding the imperfections in ourselves and also in those we encounter, will guide our steps further down that path to forgiveness, friendship, freedom and fulfillment. It is my intention that the examples given throughout this book will reveal areas in our lives where we have: taken Jesus off the throne and replaced Him with others, allowed others to mistreat us under the guise of submission to religious authority, accepted false teachings as truth, abdicated our personal responsibility to study Scripture and neglected to develop our own relationship with the Holy Spirit.

Abused by the Church will also recount stories of those who were taken advantage of and left permanently disillusioned. Other incidents will be related about individuals who, though once disappointed, forgave and profited from their mistakes and the errors of others. Examples will be given of those who served purely for the love of Jesus and were greatly blessed. This work would not be complete without the accounts of dedicated leaders who suffered rejection and neglect at the hands of those they served.

In order for victims to become victors, their stories need to be told… *"There is a time for everything, and a season for every activity under heaven: a time to be silent and a time to speak," (Ecclesiastes 3: 1, 7).*

"To Be Forewarned Is To Be Forearmed!"

"Son of man, I have made you a watchman for the house of Israel; so hear the word I speak and give them warning from me" (Ezekiel 3:17).

"My brothers, if one of you should wander from the truth and someone should bring him back, remember this: Whoever turns a sinner from the error of his way will save him from death and cover over a multitude of sins" (James 5:19-20).

"The ordinances of the Lord are sure and altogether righteous. By them is your servant warned; in keeping them there is a great reward" (Psalm 19:9, 11).

Chapter One

Warnings Heeded or Ignored

Engraved in the memories of all who lived through the horrors of the aftermath of Hurricane Katrina are graphic images of horrors too unimaginable to ever forget. Hour after hour we watched as the media brought us pictures of desperate people stranded on flooded roof-tops. Mothers were heard pleading for food and water for their starving babies. Masses were observed screaming for someone to rescue them from violent marauders who attacked them while they gathered in the Convention Center. Hungry, dehydrated, buffeted by the winds and driving rains, many were photographed holding up signs begging for help. Nursing home patients abandoned in their beds with no hope of surviving the rising flood waters were left to drown. Pet owners at every shelter were observed weeping uncontrollably for their beloved pets left behind in their submersed homes. Nurses and doctors in flooded hospitals told their heart wrenching stories of how they tried desperately to save the lives of those critically ill patients who needed life support equipment to survive.

For those of us viewing these dreadful scenes on the news, but being completely powerless to do anything to rescue these people, it was unbearable. Hour after hour, day after day, our nation watched and heard the screams and cries of the victims of this disaster cling to life. Even worse was the undeniable knowledge that many suffered and many died; and it could have been prevented.

Warnings were given but many did not heed them. Days before the storm hit, the National Weather Service broadcasted declarations that a major hurricane was bearing down on Louisiana. People in the coastal areas were repeatedly warned to evacuate. Thousands ignored the government officials' continual advice to leave their homes. Mistakenly, they did not believe that the storm was as ferocious as was being reported. Others thought it would not strike their region. Many had successfully weather other hurricanes through the years and thought that Katrina would be no different. Some people had no place to run away to or lacked the finances necessary to escape. Numerous individuals had no transportation out of the city and were trapped there by their circumstances.

Those who heeded the warnings were spared the agony Katrina brought to their neighbors. Though they lost their property, they did not suffer the misery of those who didn't evacuate. Amidst all the cries of incompetence at the way the government handled the catastrophe, no one accused the national or local officials that there were insufficient warnings given.

Grave Consequences Follow Abuse

Just like the terrible suffering endured by observing the suffering of the victims of Katrina's wrath, we often watch as people about us suffer at the hands of others. Time and time again we warn, but frequently the warnings go unheeded. Unable to convince them that they are in danger, we are force to stand by helplessly and watch their demise.

This is a picture of what has been happening to many in the Christian community. The frustration we experience is real, as real as when we watched powerlessly while people suffered at the hands of Katrina's flood waters. Seeing their loved ones taken advantage of by ministers of the gospel has brought many to the point of desperation. Helplessly, they have observed their associates suffer needlessly. They have watched these church members lose their finances at the hands of unscrupulous church officials, spend long hours volunteering at church while neglecting their responsibilities at home, have no time left to care for or visit their ageing parents, and incur great debt by taking out loans to pay their church pledges. Some have been stunned to hear that their friends or family member have even remortgage their homes at their minister's request and donated the proceeds to the latest building fund.

Ultimately, many of those who gave so flagrantly to build what they thought was God's kingdom found that they could not afford the debt they incurred. After many months of struggling to pay their bills, some went into foreclosure, while others found it necessary to sell their homes. In order to make ends meet, congregants were seen working a second or even a third job. Heartache and frustration filled those who knew all this suffering was unnecessary. It could have been easily avoided, if their friends had listened to their warnings.

Those who spent inordinate hours of time serving at the church were affected just as adversely as those who gave exorbitantly of their financial support. Heartbroken acquaintances watched them devote most evenings at the church either volunteering to help with construction projects, teaching classes, leading prayer meetings, or practicing for worship or other performances. Saturdays were spent working on the church grounds or involved in outreach events. None of these activities were wrong for the church member to be involved in. But it was wrong to spend an inordinate amount of time serving in this capacity at the expense of other relationships.

Our first responsibility is to God, then to our family, and third to our church family. When asked which the greatest commandment was, "*Jesus replied: 'Love the Lord your God with all your heart and with all your soul and with all your mind.' This is the first and greatest commandment. And the second is like it: 'Love your neighbor as yourself'" (Matthew 22:37-39).* Loving God should not be confused with serving at the church. Only when led by the Holy Spirit—and done out of love for Him—is this an act of love of God.

In spite of the repeated warnings from people who cared, dire consequences fell upon those who disregarded their wise advice. Marriages were devastated, children neglected, extended family members overlooked and friends outside the church forgotten. The once intimate relationship they had with their Lord was now exchanged for a grueling religious walk.

Immorality Cloaked In Christianity

Perhaps the worst infractions have been demonstrated by those who have committed adultery and used their position in the church to validate, hide or even justify it. Many members of religious congregation have been victimized by the overt sexual advances of their overseers. Vulnerable because of the prominence these leaders took in their lives, they succumbed to the temptations their advances offered.

The greatest tragedies have occurred when children and even adults were molested. To use ones position as a representative of Christ to victimize others is an unspeakable travesty against Christianity. Headlines in the news trumpet these injustices and make a mockery of religion.

Women and children have been paraded before us as victims of religious sects who adhere to the unlawful practice of polygamy. Pictures of twelve and thirteen year old girls forced to marry old men have brought tears to the hearts of multitudes as we watched helplessly. In spite of the government's attempts to stop this unlawful practice, it continues. Innocent people are brainwashed because the truths in Scripture are twisted, and they are led to believe fallacies.

Jan and Larry's Story

"Jan! Listen to me. That man is taking advantage of you. I have a really bad feeling about him," Jan's mother warned. "Pray about having him stay at your home," she pleaded. Though she knew that her mom had a keen sense of discernment, Jan ignored her words of caution. After all, Jan reasoned, what did she know about the minister that she and her husband had recently met at a church conference and opened their home to?

Even though Jan's mother was an avid intercessor, a respected elder in her own church, and someone whose opinion she usually trusted, Jan reasoned she was wrong this time. This man, who had come from a foreign country as a missionary to the USA, had a long list of credentials. Many people had been helped by his ministry already; and he had only been in town for a few weeks. Jan and Larry felt that the success he was having when he prayed for people was proof enough that God was endorsing His ministry. Furthermore, they were convinced that someone who wore the title he had and was an ordained pastor must be legitimate and honorable.

Just four months later, Jan and Larry deeply regretted their decision to discount Jan's mother's wise advice. And so the tragic story of abuse and indoctrination unfolded. Because he had no place to stay, this kindhearted couple hosted the pastor. They allowed him to come and live in their home with the understanding that he could stay there for a few weeks free of charge until he found an apartment. Soon after his arrival, Larry found the minister a building to rent for church services. Many people began to come to the new church; and in a month the budding church grew to fifty members. All appeared to be going well until one fateful day.

Because both Jan and Larry were members of the board of directors for this fledgling church, the new pastor asked Jan to bring him to his accountant's office. It was during that eye-opening meeting, that Jan realized what her discerning mother was trying to warn her about. The missionary was determined to get the accountant and the board of directors of the church to submit to his demands for his budget requirements. The request he made for his salary was one hundred percent of what the church collected. The accountant and Jan explained that that was unreasonable and illegal. No matter how they reiterated that there would be no funds left to pay any of the other church's expenses, the adamant pastor vehemently insisted that his salary be met. In spite of the fact that there would be no money to support the children's ministry, rent for their building, office expenses or missions, he stubbornly refused to adjust his demands.

Returning home from this upsetting meeting, Jan realized that this man was not what he portrayed himself to be. For five months, Larry and Jan had wholeheartedly welcomed him into their home and supported him as best they could. Now, not only had he been intimidating and avaricious at the meeting with the accountant, but he had treated Jan with great contempt as well.

To make matters worse, upon arriving home from their meeting with the accountant, he made another demand. Calling a meeting of the leaders, he asked the five month old church to buy him a new high-end vehicle. When Larry and Jan and a few other members of the board of directors calmly and respectfully explained that this was unreasonable, they were all asked to resign immediately from the board.

Knowing that many of the congregants were attending the church because Jan and Larry had endorsed this missionary, they felt deeply responsible for the care of these innocent people. Instinctively, Jan and Larry knew that a leader with these character flaws would wound those attending his church.

At this point the pastor moved from their home. Despite his many attempts to meet with the pastor to confront him with his misgivings over his actions, Larry was rebuffed and his requests for a meeting went ignored.

Concern for those attending the church welled within their hearts. Larry and Jan had no recourse—no way to warn the congregation of the impending and inevitable abuse that would be sure to follow. All they could do was pray and be honest with those who inquired about why they left the church. Some called and some stopped by to listen to their advice. But, most of the church members stayed and discounted their warnings.

Helplessly, Larry and Jan watched as the inevitable occurred. Families were split and emotionally wounded over the pastor's harsh teachings. Generous, caring couples were taken advantage of—just like Jan and Larry were. Gradually, one by one, people saw what was happening, and after a few years they all left the church. The missionaries' bills for his luxurious car and various other expenses were paid for by the few leaders who took responsibility for his actions.

The spiritual, emotional and financial abuse that transpired could have been avoided if the wise warnings given were heeded and not ignored. If each one had taken the time to pray and listen to the Holy Spirit, so much pain would have been avoided. Instead, of studying the Scriptures, Jan, Larry and the other church members filled their time with frantic service and hours of ministry. Blinded by ignorance, they took God off His rightful place in their lives and allowed this man to reside there.

Jesus Confronts Abuse and Deception

A similar situation of the control and abuse of authority was happening two thousand years ago when Jesus taught in Jerusalem. The religious leaders were making demands of the people over and above their tithe and far more than what God required of them. *Jesus replied, "And you experts in the law, woe to you, because you load people down with heavy burdens they can hardly carry, and you yourselves will not lift one finger to help them" (Luke 11:46).*

They presented their rules in such a way that they negated the laws of God. The people were intimidated into following their teachings for fear of offending God. Addressing the Pharisees and teachers of the law, *"Jesus replied, 'And why do you break the command of God for the sake of your tradition? For God said, 'Honor your father and mother'....But you say that if a man says to his father or mother, 'Whatever help you might otherwise have received from me is a gift devoted to God,' he is not to honor his father with it. Thus you nullify the word of God for the sake of your tradition. You hypocrites!" (Matthew 15:3-7).*

Jesus warned those oppressed by the religious leaders to evacuate! *"Leave them; they are blind guides. If a blind man leads a blind man both will fall into the pit" (Matthew*

15:14). He told them that their leaders were expecting too much from them and, even worse, were not leading them to heaven. His warning was specific when he explained that if they continued to follow the erroneous teachings of their current leaders, they would meet the same fate as their blind guides. *"For I tell you that unless your righteousness surpasses that of the Pharisees and the teachers of the law, you will certainly not enter the kingdom of heaven" (Matthew 5:20).*

Jesus warned that not everyone is to be trusted just because they are a minister and proclaim they are teaching the truth of God's Word: *"'But be on your guard against the yeast of the Pharisees and the Sadducees.' Then they understood that he was not telling them to guard against the yeast used in bread, but against the teaching of the Pharisees and Sadducees" (Matthew 16:11-12).*

These were the religious leaders of Jesus' day, but the warning remains for us today to guard ourselves against being deceived. In order to know what the will of God for our lives is truly, we must read the Bible ourselves and not depend totally on someone else for our spiritual direction. He has given us leaders to train us and teach us His ways; but that does not mean that we have no responsibility to acquire understanding and knowledge ourselves. Paul explained this truth to Timothy: *"All Scripture is God breathed and is useful for teaching, rebuking, correcting and training in righteousness, so that the man of God may be thoroughly equipped for* every good work" *(2 Timothy 3:16)*. If we know the Word of God and spend intimate time with the Holy Spirit, we can avoid the pitfalls of deception and be equipped to help others.

Erroneous Philosophies Followed

Many congregants blindly obey because they are indoctrinated to believe that if they do not submit to their leaders, they are not obeying God. During Sunday sermons, they have been mistakenly taught that they don't have to pray about what the pastor asks of them. Many have been led to believe that just because the pastor asks for their commitment to his cause, it is God's will that they submit and obey. Even in regards to giving financial offerings, some are coaxed that they don't need to pray about it: "Just give and God will bless you." Guilt is often used to manipulate the congregants to go into debt for the sake of the church. If they spend long hours serving daily at the church, they are taught that God will bless their families. They would discern the error in this doctrine and ignore it, if they knew what the Bible taught. Instead, they frequently fall into the trap of following the erroneous philosophies presented to them.

Sometimes candidly, other times quite subtly, many of these church members are warned by concerned family members to reevaluate their dedication to their church. Frequently, those cautioned are told that the level of control by the church involved is disproportionate to what Scripture intends. Sadly, most of these well-intentioned warnings have gone unheeded.

The Holy Spirit Guides All Who Heed

One of the most effective ways the Holy Spirit frequently speaks to us is through the Scriptures. Other times, God leads us through our acquaintances, as well as through those He places over us to teach and instruct us in His Word. I cannot stress enough that in order to discern when it is the Holy Spirit guiding us, and to avoid being deceived, we must know the Scriptures ourselves. One such Scripture teaches us that our leader must be: *"...hospitable, one who loves what is good, who is self-controlled, upright, holy and disciplined. He must hold firmly to the trustworthy message as it has been taught, so that he can encourage others by sound doctrine and refute those who oppose it" (Titus 1:8-9).* To neglect the Word, sets us in the place where we can be easily duped.

Paul left specific guidelines of the qualifications we should see in those appointed to lead us: *"An elder must be blameless, the husband of but one wife, a man whose children believe and are not open to the charge of being wild and disobedient. Since an overseer is entrusted with God's work, he must be blameless—not overbearing, not quick-tempered, not given to drunkenness, not violent, not pursuing dishonest gain" (Titus 1:6-7).* Using Scriptures like this, the

Holy Spirit nudges those who read these instructions out of deception into the truth.

Scripture has been given to us to warn us, guide us in our daily walk, and instruct us in the way to live a wise life. If we are too busy to take the time to read and meditate on His Word, we will not be positioned to receive the clear warnings that the Holy Spirit wants to deliver to us. Time and time again, Scripture teaches us to seek God about all of our decisions. *"I will lead the blind by ways they have not known, along unfamiliar paths I will guide them; I will turn the darkness into light before them and make the rough places smooth" (Isaiah 42:16).*

In 1 Samuel 8 God's instruction is clear that we should never look to a man to rule over our lives. *"..they have rejected me as their king...forsaking me and serving other gods" (1 Samuel 8:7-8).* Back in the days of the prophet Samuel, the Israelites cried out to God for a king to lead them. God wanted to be their King. But they wanted a king they could physically see, audibly hear and follow. God surrendered to their request and gave them a king. This king ruled with an iron fist. Like Israel, many in our day, have exchanged their personnel relationship with their God for a hard taskmaster.

Going to God daily to seek His advice and guidance keeps Him in the place of ruling. It also affords us the protection of not allowing another person to take control of our lives to benefit them. Hearing His voice in the Scriptures, as well as listening to that still small voice within us, is His way. If we follow Him and listen and obey His directives, we will never fall into the trap of being deceived by another.

God will never take advantage of us. He will never treat us like slaves. We are His children and His friends. It breaks His heart when He sees us ignore His warnings and fall into the trap of being abused by some of the leaders of His church.

The Fate of the Victims of Abuse

After a season of serving a demanding leader the inevitable happens. The victims are left much like those who ignored the warning of the approaching hurricane. Alone and afraid, the flood waters of disappointment and opposition threaten to engulf them. Through the years, I have heard the account of many who were warned, like Jan and Larry, that the leaders they were following were overstepping their bounds. Excessive demands were being placed on their time and their finances. Friends, coworkers, and relatives warned but were unfortunately ignored. They did not evacuate and run for safer ground.

The level of control escalated until the hapless victims could not deny it. Once they did, they were left like the victims in the flood waters of Katrina, sitting on the rooftop of their broken lives-desperate, abandoned and dejected. Hungry for the truth, dehydrated from not receiving the living water of His presence; their condition became dire.

Caution:

"The Signs and Symptoms
Of
Emotional Abuse!"

"...they have rejected me as their king...warn them solemnly and let them know what the king who will reign over them will do" (1 Samuel 8:7, 9).

"No man can redeem the life of another or give to God a ransom for him—" (Psalm 49:7).

"This is the fate of those who trust in themselves, and of their followers, who approve their sayings... The upright will rule over them in the morning; their forms will decay in the grave, far from their princely mansions" (Psalm 49:13-14).

"...Never again will an oppressor overrun my people, for now I am keeping watch" (Zechariah 9:8).

Chapter Two

The Pain of Abuse

Searing pain ripped across Mary's chest. Perspiration beaded her brow while Mary's heart raced uncontrollably within her chest. Was she experiencing a sudden heart attack as she prepared to go to bed? It had been an especially trying day, ending with a troubling leadership meeting at church. Tired but in good health, she could not understand where this sudden explosion of pain came from. Mary had not suffered from heart disease and was in excellent condition for a woman her age. Sitting down trying to catch her breath, Mary realized that she had felt the same pain another time in her life.

Alone with her thoughts and the unexpected pain, Mary recalled a time when someone she was very close to had wounded her emotionally. Riveted by the memory of this very painful time in her life, Mary suddenly realized that she was once again feeling abused by someone she trusted and loved.

On this eventful evening, during a leadership class, the pastor used this occasion to indirectly present a strong criticism against Mary and her husband, Joe. Feeling that their decision to launch their own ministry was an act of rebellion, their pastor taught a class on the downfalls of pursuing an independent ministry. Joe and Mary were convinced that the Lord had led them to launch their own ministry to help the poor and underprivileged. Deeply wounded that they weren't confronted privately by their pastor with his concerns, they returned home from their class very disturbed. His veiled stern rebuke tore at their hearts.

Shockingly, it took the physical pain Mary was enduring for her and Joe to realize that they were being mistreated. Abuse is like that for some of us. Almost like quicksand, we step into it quite unexpectedly and are ensnared by its ability to sap us of our joy, strength, independence and even our life. The pain of rejection, the overwhelming trap of being controlled, the fear of being persecuted can actually bring physical symptoms much like Mary was experiencing.

Once this couple realized that they were caught in a cycle of abuse, Mary and Joe determined to confront the individuals and put a stop to it immediately. Feeling like she was in control of her life once again, slowly the painful symptoms subsided.

Joe and Mary often related that they wished that the abuse they suffered came from a government agency, a difficult friend or a stubborn relative. Any of these would have been easier for them to deal with and would have brought much less unrest.

For many years Joe and Mary had been very active leaders in their church. This was a place of solace and deep inspiration. For years, they had been taught and trained to serve God's people there. To their dismay, it was this church and these leaders, that they were so connected to, that had begun to mistreat them. They were aware that it was not the pastors' intentions to harm them, nor was it his plan to bring so much suffering into their lives, but that is what happened.

Over a course of time, Mary and Joe had assumed many responsibilities within the church and developed a close rapport with the congregation. Friendly with hundreds of wonderful people, they enjoyed the time they spent ministering and praying for each and every one of them. Daily Mary or Joe could be found at the church: praying for the leaders, helping with construction projects, teaching Bible studies, or leading teams out to minister in the prison and to nursing homes. Serving at the church had become their whole life. Nothing was as important to them, nor did anything in their lives get in the way of their fulfilling their obligations to God's people.

The church and its people had become more significant to Mary and Joe than the God that they were devoted to and serving. Slowly, unobtrusively, they had lost their first love and replaced it with a counterfeit. Serving God's church and His people had taken first place in their lives and pushed their Friend out of the central place that He had previously held.

Mary and Joe began to realize that they had exchanged their King for another and were now serving a hard taskmaster. When they didn't meet up to the expectations of those they were serving, their pastors' displeasure and rejection became unbearable. After all, these church leaders were everything to Mary and Joe; and now their pastors did not approve of the direction they were going.

Feeling led by God to the missions, Mary's and Joe's pursuit of this calling was seen as an act of rebellion. Placed in direct conflict with what they knew God was leading them to do and opposed to what the leaders wanted, they had to make a choice. Who would be their true king? Could Joe and Mary exchange the applause of man for the favor of their God? Were they willing to lose all they had worked for, to please Him that they professed to serve? After much prayer, this courageous couple's choice was to leave all: their positions of leadership, their friends, those they taught and cared for—and follow their God.

This decision launched the sting of retribution from the church that they loved and served so faithfully. People they had devotedly served and taught were no longer allowed to have any contact with them. Fearful that they would turn

members away from the church by exposing their griev-
ances, they were depicted by the leaders as an evil influence. Portrayed as a couple who had a spirit of rebellion,
all their former acquaintances shunned them for fear of
being contaminated by their rebelliousness. Even a simple
trip to the supermarket became unbearable. Watching previously close friends avoid them by running away when they
saw them in the store pierced Mary's and Joe's hearts with
sorrow.

The abuse did not just keep itself contained within the
members of the church but manifested in other venues as
well. A short time after leaving the church, Mary was asked
to preach to a gathering of Christian businessmen. They had
heard her testimony at another event and felt led to ask Mary
to relate her experiences as a missionary to Western Europe to
those attending their next gathering. Days before the scheduled event, Mary received a call that revealed how insidious
the attack she was experiencing had become. Apologizing
for the change in plans, the gentleman from the Christian
association nervously cancelled her speaking engagement.
One of the pastors from the church they had left approached
the minister in charge of the event and asked that Mary be
removed from the itinerary. In order for this to happen, Mary
and Joe were sure that they had been portrayed in a very
disparaging light.

Removing the Plank

Shunned, slandered, and deeply wounded by those who were closest to them, Mary and Joe began to realize that the abuse they were suffering was partly of their own making. *"Why do you look at the speck of sawdust in your brother's eye and pay no attention to the plank in your own eye (Matthew 7:3)?* Led by His Word, they began to take their focus off those who had hurt them and started to take a good look at their own lives.

They recognized that they had left the protective confines of His heart and given their hearts to another. Mary and Joe had become like Israel when they sought after a king. God was not enough for them. They wanted a man to honor and serve. Subtly they, too, had fallen into the same trap. Looking for a good, godly leader was not wrong; but looking for someone to place on a pedestal to exalt was. Allowing others to lead them, instead of relying on God to continually show them the way, had opened Mary and Joe up to the abuse of man.

Alone with their King, no longer able to communicate with those who had become their life, Mary and Joe set out on the path of following Jesus, not men. During their time alone with the Lord, He once again began to teach them His ways. Little by little He healed the wounds of abuse, removed the scars of rejection and helped them to forgive everyone, including themselves.

Mary and Joe are not alone in falling into the trap of idolatry. Attempting to obey the Lord's command to love, this couple and many others like them, have twisted it into exactly what He had commanded everyone not to do—worshipping others. *"Jesus answered, 'It is written: 'Worship the Lord your God and serve him only'" (Luke 4:8).*

In Search Of a King

Deep within most people is a desire to set someone upon a pedestal and worship them. Many of us are looking for heroes or idols to worship. From the youngest children to the elderly, most of us have men or women that we highly esteem. Whenever one of these elect individuals falls from grace and commits a travesty, there is a great scandal. We walk around hanging our heads in disappointment. But before long, we once again begin searching for someone else to emulate. *"...Therefore the people wander like sheep oppressed for lack of a shepherd" (Zechariah 10: 2).*

Inherit in all of us is a need to worship and to find someone to imitate. This is the case because we were created to worship God and look up to Him as our Father and role model. We are not satisfied unless each of us achieves the purpose for which we were made. Worshipping God and trying to love like Him is the greatest thing we can do. To replace Him with another is a terrible reduction of our aspirations and a travesty against God. He alone is worthy to be worshipped and followed. Setting a man upon that special seat of honor and excluding God from the place of ruling in our lives is contrary to His plan for us and will only lead to difficulties.

Many times this adulation of another person leads us to aspire to the greatness we see in them. Motivation to better ourselves can slip into a dangerous spirit of jealousy, if we are not very careful. This insidious attack of jealousy does not just limit itself to the common man. History has shown us that many a leader has also succumbed to the temptation that jealousy presented to them through those they perceived as more astute than them. Overcome by envy, all the good they had accomplished in their lives was destroyed and brought havoc on the people whom they ruled.

History Reveals the Weaknesses of Men

The story of the Israelites desire for a king as told in 1Samuel 8 in the Old Testament is a perfect example of how disastrous it can be for those who long for someone to idolize. Surrounded by nations that had kings ruling over them, Israel jealously looked upon these nations and cried out to God for a king like theirs. Speaking emphatically, God told His prophet, Samuel, "*'...they have rejected me as their king...warn them solemnly and let them know what the king who will reign over them will do'*" (1 Samuel 8:7,9).

The Lord then listed a litany of problems they would most assuredly encounter if they continued to pursue their demand for a king to rule over them. Their children would have to serve as: foot soldiers, commanders in the military, farmers of his land, blacksmiths, perfumers, bakers and cooks. He warned them that the new king would take the best of their fields and property, a tenth of their grain and their flocks, as well as their servants and donkeys. He also cautioned them that they would become the king's slaves.

In spite of these stern warnings spoken through the prophet, Samuel, the people refused to listen. They continued to demand that they wanted a king to lead them and to go out before them in battle.

Sometimes God will surrender to our persistent requests, even if they are not in our best interest. This was the case for Israel. God told Samuel to give them a king.

The person that God chose was *"Saul, an impressive young man without equal among the Israelites—a head taller than any of the others" (1 Samuel 9:2)*. When Samuel called Saul forward in front of the entire nation of Israel, this thirty year old man hid among the baggage. Saul was humble and had many great qualities. He was forgiving, served his father wholeheartedly, assembled the nation to war when threatened by their enemies and was obedient to his God.

A Kind King Becomes a Tyrant

But years later, after experiencing great success as a leader and receiving the constant adulation of the people, he changed. Saul flagrantly disobeyed God's specific laws and directives, demonstrating that he considered himself above the law. When confronted by Samuel, the prophet, he made excuses for his behavior: *"'I was afraid of the people and so I gave in to them'" (1 Samuel 15:24).* He showed no humility and a complete lack of integrity in the decisions he was making. Pride motivated his actions. He became increasingly demanding, even requiring his entire army to go without food while in battle, until he avenged himself on his enemies. No longer was he serving the people, but they were his pawns executing his commands without question. The good of the people and concern for his own family were no longer prompting his actions, but selfish ambition and pride were.

The tremendous deterioration in his character manifested fully when a teenage boy arrived on the scene. This youth, David, a lowly shepherd, single-handedly killed the nine-foot tall giant, Goliath. The Philistines led by Goliath were threatening to enslave Israel. Armed with a sling-shot, David felled the giant, precipitating a great victory for Israel. From that day on, David led the troops in many successful campaigns and won the praises of the people. Much to King Saul's displeasure, the adulation that once was his now had to be shared with David. Scripture declares, *"And from that time on Saul kept a jealous eye on David" (1 Samuel 18: 9).*

As time progressed so did the jealousy that consumed Saul. A deep hatred for David overtook the king. Time and time again, he tried unsuccessfully to kill David. Soon David had to leave his community and flee for his life. Even the young man's departure didn't stop the relentless Saul from pursuing him. One murderous scheme after another marked the remainder of his reign.

Where was the once humble, kindhearted king - the man God said was small in his own eyes? This unassuming man years later set up a monument on Mt Carmel in his own honor. What became of the man the people mandated to lead them? It appeared that his regal position and the excessive adoration of the people changed the once servant-like king into a murderous tyrant. No longer was Saul concerned for the good of the nation and its people. Motivated by selfish-ambition and pride, controlled by hatred, and separated from his God, his reign ended in complete failure.

Israel's eagerly sought after king brought them many problems and hardships and left them disillusioned. Anyone we permit to rule indiscriminately over our lives will do the same to us. Like Israel, we will enjoy a short period of reveling in the charismatic strength of our new king, until we see and experience their innate weaknesses. Then the task of living as a subject under the domain of a domineering, counterfeit king will be ours. History shows us that worshipping a man ruins him—and us.

The overbearing king in our lives could be anyone or anything that we love and honor more than God. It might be a person, a thing, a place, an ideology, a church, a religion, a political party, a politician....

Knowingly or unknowingly, we may place someone on His throne and worship them. Leaders, churches, men or women can become hazardous to our spiritual growth and our emotional health, if we give them disproportionate authority to rule over our lives and the worship that belongs to God alone. It is time for the people of God to let Him reign once again as our king and lord. *"Never again will an oppressor overrun my people, for now I am keeping watch"* *(Zechariah 9:8).*

"The Greatest of All Is the Servant of All!"

"Do nothing out of selfish ambition or vain conceit, but in humility consider others better than your-selves. Each of you should look not only to your own interests, but also to the interests of others. Your atti-tude should be the same as that of Christ Jesus: Who, being in very nature God, did not consider equality with God something to be grasped, but made himself nothing, taking the very nature of a servant.." *(Philippians 2:3-7).*

"...Instead, whoever wants to become great among you must be your servant, and whoever wants to be first must be your slave—just as the Son of Man did not come to be served, but to serve, and to give his life as a ransom for many'" *(Matthew 20: 26-28).*

Chapter Three

Jesus' Leadership Plan

Aprominent evangelist was scheduled to speak at a local church. Prior to his arrival a long list of expectations was sent to the hosting church. The list included: the type of car that was to be used to pick him up at the airport, the highest quality hotel was to be provided, exact specifications for him and his families' meals had to be adhered to- including the brand of water they were given to drink, a substantial offering was required. All these demands were met; a very successful crusade occurred; but this ministry was never invited to return. In spite of the level of the anointing on his prophetic ministry, the cost of caring for him and his family far outshone the benefits.

The hosting church always treated their visiting ministry with great hospitality. Their level of appreciation was evidenced by the generous offerings they gave all who served them as well as the lavish hospitality they extended to them. This they felt was their obligation and never resented being generous towards those who came to minister at their church. In this case though, the demands the evangelist made of them were disproportionate and excessive.

It appeared that this minister forgot who he was following. Would Jesus have demanded to be treated as a celebrity? Would He have required so much effort and financial support to be extended to Him and His friends?

This was not the way Jesus conducted His very successful ministry. *"Do nothing out of selfish ambition or vain conceit, but in humility consider others better than yourselves. Each of you should look not only to your own interests, but also to the interests of others. Your attitude should be the same as that of Christ Jesus: Who, being in very nature God, did not consider equality with God something to be grasped, but made himself nothing, taking the very nature of a servant.."* *(Philippians 2:3-7)*. This Scripture verse explains the balance we should all strive to maintain in our relationships, either as leaders or as congregants.

Our understanding of success and prominence is often clouded by the examples we observe about us. Watching politicians, successful businessman, and wealthy entrepreneurs treated with great acclaim, we might begin to believe that leading others would afford us the same significance.

Qualifications for Leadership

Instead of looking to the world for the qualifications of a successful leader, we must examine the example and teachings that Jesus gave us on this controversial subject. One day the mother of James and John came to Jesus and asked, *"Grant that one of these two sons of mine may sit at your right and the other at your left in your kingdom" (Matthew 20:23)*

When the ten apostles heard that the son's of Zebedee had tried to get a high position in Jesus' kingdom, they were indignant. Secretly, they were wishing that they would be chosen to hold that special place of ruling beside Jesus. Knowing what was in the heart of each of these men: *"Jesus called them together and said, 'You know that the rulers of the Gentiles lord it over them, and their high officials exercise authority over them. Not so with you. Instead, whoever wants to become great among you must be your servant, and whoever wants to be first must be your slave—just as the Son of Man did not come to be served, but to serve, and to give his life as a ransom for many'" (Matthew 20: 25-28).* The Lord taught His position seeking disciples that they must serve others if they would achieve stature in His kingdom.

He demonstrated this important principle by washing the feet of His disciples—not the common job of a king. During the Passover Feast, on the night before He suffered and died for mankind, Jesus showed His apostles how He wanted them to conduct themselves toward others: *"...so he got up from the meal, took off his outer clothing, and wrapped a towel around his waist. After that, he poured water into a basin and began to wash his disciples' feet, drying them with the towel that was wrapped around him....*

"When he had finished washing their feet, he put on his clothes and returned to his place. 'Do you understand what I have done for you?' He asked them. 'You call me 'Teacher' and 'Lord' and rightly so, for that is what I am. Now that I, your Lord and Teacher, have washed your feet, you also should wash one another's feet. I have set you an example that you should do as I have done for you'" *(John 13:4-5,12-15)*. Knowing that He had very little time left on earth, He wanted to make sure that they fully understood what being a leader in His kingdom meant. If He, their Messiah, could attend others with such love and humility, then they should follow His example and serve His people enthusiastically as well.

Motivated To Serve Jesus

Earlier Jesus stated clearly, *"...Worship the Lord your God, and serve him only"* *(Matthew 4:10)*. Both in His discourse with James and John's mother and the disciples, and by the example He set by washing the feet of His apostles, Jesus taught that we must serve others, too. Comparing these scriptures with the following verse from Ephesians, it is clear that Jesus wants us to serve because we love Him and never turn that service into worshipping anyone but God. *"Serve wholeheartedly, as if you were serving the Lord, not men, because you know that the Lord will reward everyone for whatever good he does..." (Ephesians 6: 7-8).*

To serve for any other motive will bring defeat into our lives and rob us of our reward. *"So whether you eat or drink or whatever you do, do it all for the glory of God" (1 Corinthians 10:31).* There are many examples in Scripture of individuals who fell into the trap of serving others for the wrong motives. Their stories will hopefully inspire us to avoid the same mistakes.

We've already seen how King Saul's motives to lead Israel out of love for God changed and became egocentric. Subtly, he began seeking after fame, fortune and power. James and John's example offer us a stern warning as well. Even though they were continually with Jesus, they fell into the temptation of desiring position and all the perks that go along with it: honor, prestige, supremacy, wealth.

Close friends of Jesus, Martha and her sister Mary, depict the contrast of doing all for Jesus or for one's own self interest. Martha opened her home to Jesus and became preoccupied with all the preparations. Meanwhile her sister, Mary, sat at the Lord's feet listening to all he said. Annoyed that her sister left her to do all the cooking and cleaning, Martha complained to Jesus. She asked Him to make Mary help with all the work. Jesus made it perfectly clear what is important to Him: *"'Martha, Martha,' the Lord answered, 'you are worried and upset about many things, but only one thing is needed. Mary has chosen what is better, and it will not be taken away from her'" (Luke 10:41-42).*

In the midst of serving Jesus, Martha lost her way. At first motivated by her devotion to Him, she soon became distracted. So subtly, she began to work and serve for the wrong motives: What would people think of her? Was her cooking of the highest standard? Did her home reflect the spotlessness of a meticulous homemaker? Ever so gently, Jesus realigned her motives back to what was truly important: doing all, and only those things that He asks her to do, for Him. He wasn't looking for excellence in her homemaking skills but wanted her loving attention. Getting her eyes off herself and her guests, and back on Jesus, was the first step back to pleasing Him.

We, like Martha, can start out serving Jesus for the right reason and ever so slowly begin to be inspired by the wrong motives. Once our eyes are off Jesus, and we become preoccupied with ourselves and pleasing those people around us, we will lose all the benefits of truly serving our King.

Letting Down the Shield

Serving purely for Jesus, offers us a shield of protection from the schemes of the enemy. Judas Iscariot was a prime example of one who fell into dire sin because he stopped serving Jesus. Motivated by his love for money, Judas, one of the twelve apostles, sold Jesus to the chief priests for thirty silver coins. His treachery led to the cruel beating and agonizing crucifixion of our Savior. His love for money superseded his devotion to Jesus. Many, like Judas, fall into the same trap of serving for selfish gain. Scripture warns: *"People who want to get rich fall into temptation and a trap and into many foolish and harmful desires that plunge men into ruin and destruction. For the love of money is a root of all kinds of evil. Some people, eager for money, have wandered from the faith and pierced themselves with many griefs" (1 Timothy 6:9-10).*

Many start out serving their congregation or church for Jesus and end up exchanging their pure motives for tainted ones. It is imperative that we check our motives on a regular basis. One of the signs that we have entered into dangerous territory is our reaction toward people when they don't show us the level of appreciation we expect for our service. If we are serving for man's approval, selfish ambition, greed or any other motive, we will be overcome with hurt and disappointment. As we saw in the lives of King Saul and Judas, these wounds, left unchecked, will fester and open us up to jealousy, bitterness, resentment, fear and hatred.

Our Father allows people to disappoint us by their reaction to our service to expose the impurity of our motives for our benefit. If we humble ourselves before Him, He will gently bring us back to wholeness. As we observed in the story of Martha, He will purify our motives with His word and turn us back to serving others for the glory of Jesus—not ourselves.

If we are serving others for love of Jesus, no matter what the response, our minds will be kept in perfect peace. *"You will keep in perfect peace him whose mind is steadfast, because he trusts in you" (Isaiah 26:3).* No matter what we do out of loving obedience to our God, we will feel His approval because He always values our service. He rewards those who diligently serve Him. One of the greatest signs of His loving approval is the manifestation of His presence. Nothing else we receive from anyone for our service compares to a few minutes in His presence.

Serve Like Jesus

It is obvious that the Lord God desires that we demonstrate our love for Him by serving one another. Whether we are ministers or members of a congregation, we are all called to serve. Problems can arise when others are serving our needs. We can begin to feel self-important and not just expect to be treated royally—but demand it. As we saw in the tragic story of Saul, he forgot that he was chosen by God to serve the people. After years of reigning as king, he thought he was too good to serve anyone—even God. We, too, can forget that no matter what our position, first and foremost, we are called by God to serve Him and our fellowman for Him.

Instead of following Saul's poor example, we must follow the balanced example that Jesus portrayed for us, if we are to be pleasing to our King. He served mankind as no other has: He fed the multitudes, healed the sick, delivered those held captive by demons, frequently taught vast crowds, and died a cruel death to pay the price for our sins. Our wonderful suffering Servant taught us by His example and by His words: *"My command is this: Love each other as I have loved you" (John 15: 12).*

Not only did Jesus serve but He allowed His disciples to serve Him as well. Mary washed His feet with her tears and anointed Him with costly perfume. Martha and Mary cooked meals for Him and His followers. Many devoted women followed Him and supported Jesus and His disciples out of their own means (see Luke 8: 1-3). Peter and John obediently prepared the Passover supper. Jesus sent the disciples in His name to heal the sick and deliver those held captive by the enemy. Peter was sent to pay the taxes for both he and Jesus. The Lord asked the disciples to distribute the loaves of bread and the fish to the thousands assembled before them and then to clean up after everyone ate.

Jesus was balanced. Jesus served and was served. For our good and for the good of one another, we must do the same. Like Saul, we could become prideful and eventually abusive to those who serve us, if we don't maintain the same balance

Jesus demonstrated. We, too, must first and foremost serve others and then allow them to serve, as the Lord directs.

Worship vs. Service

Leaders and congregations are both commanded to serve each other- not worship one another. Worship is excessive or ardent admiration of another person or thing, while service is merely assistance or benefit afforded to someone. It is extremely easy to fall into the insidious trap of worshipping those we admire and serve. Gradually we can begin to think too highly of these individuals. To avoid this we must frequently redirect our thoughts back to our Lord. Spending more time in His presence adoring Him and reading His Word are the best antidotes to worshipping another. Periodically reminding ourselves that these individuals are human just like we are and have faults and failings, too, offers us a shield of safety against idolizing them.

Another way we might become vulnerable to worshipping a leader is by expecting too much of them. While observing the good that they have done, we can begin to expect that they will rescue us and even be instrumental in changing our lives. God alone is able to accomplish these things for us. To rely on a leader or a body of believers for our needs to be met, is giving them the place that belongs to our Savior. He rescues the oppressed, sets the captives free and provides everything for those who lack. Jesus told His disciples, *"Consider the ravens: They do not sow or reap, they have no storeroom or barn; yet God feeds them. And how much more valuable you are than birds...Consider how the lilies grow. They do not labor or spin. Yet I tell you, not even Solomon in all his splendor was dressed like one of these. If that is how God clothes the grass of the field, which is here today, and tomorrow is thrown into the fire, how much more will he clothe you"(Luke 12:24, 27-28).*

Yes, it is true that it is part of His wonderful design to use mankind to bless us, teach us and help us get free from the oppression of the enemy. He commanded His disciples: *"Go into all the world and preach the good news to all creation. And these signs will accompany those who believe: In my name they will drive out demons; ...they will place their hands on sick people, and they will get well" (Mark 16:15,17-8).* Though this is one of the ways that He helps us, we must never attribute those accomplishments to that person, but to the God that uses them to bless others. To God be the glory for all He does—not to the people He wondrously flows through. These men and women are just instruments in His hand, used by Him to bring Him glory. Always directing our thoughts back to Him—let us remember to thank God for using them to help us. In that way, we are keeping Him on the throne in our lives and at the same time appreciating those who allow Him to use their lives to bless us.

Spending an excessive amount of time with these leaders—or desiring to do so—will propel us into the realm of worship and out of the safe-zone of service. We must allow our King to direct our steps. He will certainly lead us on the straight path of devotion to Him and away from the dangers of obsession with another. Disappointments will undoubtedly be averted if we follow His leading.

Also, it is important to avoid becoming preoccupied with thoughts of these gifted people. These thoughts can be praiseworthy or critical. Both will have the same effect of ensnaring us into inordinately worshipping someone other than God. To prevent this, it is important to keep a guard over ones thoughts. Scripture reminds us: *"Finally, brothers, whatever is true, whatever is noble, whatever is pure, whatever is lovely, whatever is admirable-if anything is praiseworthy-think about such things" (Philippians 4:8).* Only our God fits these qualifications! Let's become preoccupied with Him instead of filling our minds with thoughts of our fellow man.

"Guidelines To Giving God's Way!"

"To the elders among you,...Be shepherds of God's flock that is under your care, serving as overseers— not because you must, but because you are willing, as God wants you to be; not greedy for money, but eager to serve; not lording it over those entrusted to you, but being examples to the flock" (1 Peter 5:1-3).

"Give, and it will be given to you. A good measure, pressed down, shaken together and running over, will be poured into your lap. For with the measure you use, it will be measured to you" (Luke 6:38).

"Remember this: Whoever sows sparingly will also reap sparingly, and whoever sows generously will also reap generously. Each man should give what he has decided in his heart to give, not reluctantly or under compulsion, for God loves a cheerful giver" (2 Corinthians 9:6-7).

Chapter Four

Giving To Our King

Sorrow hid behind the eyes of the gentleman who sat across from us. My husband and I saw it peak out and then quickly retreat. Though its appearance was transient, it was unmistakably present. Tom tried unsuccessfully to hide his anguish. Amidst the intense pain this old memory engendered, Tom began to share his heartrending story.

Many years ago he and his wife attended a church near their home. A new pastor was assigned to lead the congregation. Tom felt an obligation to help this man of God with the work with as much diligence as he could. Once Tom was taught the Biblical principle of tithing (giving God ten percent of his income) he embraced it wholeheartedly. Giving seemed to come as second nature to Tom. Soon the pastor began to ask for help with other expenses the church accrued. Tom did not hesitate to give all he could. Building funds were readily embraced by Tom and given to sacrificially as well. It was common for Tom to give sacrificial offerings far above his weekly tithe on a regular basis to his church.

After many years of serving this minister of the Gospel and his church, Tom discovered a terrible secret. This man of God had been courting Tom's wife behind his back. Tom was devastated. The pastor had seduced his unsuspecting wife and drew her into an illicit affair. Once they were discovered, both the pastor and Tom's wife ran off together leaving Tom and the church floundering in the ashes of despair.

Tom was not only victimized by having his young wife taken from him, but because he had been a generous and valiant supporter of the offending pastor, the feeling of being taken advantage of was devastating. Giving unreservedly to every cause and serving the needs of the congregation had become his lifestyle. Because his level of commitment was so profound, the level of suffering he endured from this abuse was equally acute.

In the ensuing years, God blessed Tom and gave him a faithful wife and many wonderful children. Not only that, but, the Lord helped him forgive both his wife and former pastor and safely reconnect with a church. Today Tom serves in a small church with as much diligence as he served in his former church.

Tragically this story of sacrificial giving and subsequent abuse has become common. Over and over reports have surfaced of people who were coerced into giving far more than God intended and then treated shamefully after their service was no longer needed. Single moms have been asked to give offerings or make pledges to building funds far above what their limited means should allow. Because of this intense pressure to give, they found themselves suffering financial hardships. The sacrifice to their children was just as difficult: Meager meals, no nourishing snacks, and many of them left alone while their moms were working second jobs to make ends meet. Families of limited means have been persuaded into taking out loans, giving up vacations, selling cars and other possessions to help their pastor accomplish his vision. When they resisted or complained, frequently, they were asked to leave the church and were shunned by all the members.

Scripture exhorts: *"To the elders among you,...Be shepherds of God's flock that is under your care, serving as overseers—not because you must, but because you are willing, as God wants you to be; not greedy for money, but eager to serve; not lording it over those entrusted to you, but being examples to the flock" (1 Peter 5:1-3).* The Word of God urges leaders to resist the temptation to use their calling to build their own kingdoms. They are warned in this passage to avoid the temptations that pride offers. Often by hiding behind the prestige of their office, some are erroneously led to increase their power and influence over others lives in order to pursue selfish gain.

Tithes and Offerings

Giving offerings over and above our tithes is the subject of this chapter. For those who believe that tithing is no longer part of the new covenant but an old covenant teaching, Jesus clarified that truth with this teaching. *"Woe to you, teachers of the law and Pharisees, you hypocrites! You give a tenth of your spices—mint, dill, and cumin. But you have neglected the more important matters of the law—justice, mercy and faithfulness. You should have practiced the latter, without neglecting the former. You blind guides (Matthew 23:23-24)!"* Jesus made it clear to them that giving God one tenth of their income—or tithing—was not to be neglected, nor were they to avoid showing love towards others. Both were expected. *"'Bring the whole tithe into the storehouse, that there may be food in my house. Test me in this,' says the Lord Almighty, 'and see if I will not throw open the floodgates of heaven and pour out so much blessing that you will not have room enough for it'"(Malachi 3:10).*

One of the most prevalent ways congregants are wounded by those in ministry is through the pressure to give sacrificial donations over and above their tithes. Jesus taught about this very subject because the teachers and Pharisees of His day were twisting the truths in Scripture for their benefit and making excessive demands of the people. *"Jesus replied, 'And you experts in the law, woe to you, because you load people down with heavy burdens they can hardly carry, and you yourselves will not lift one finger to help them'" (Luke 11:46).* The Pharisees were encouraging the people to hold back the support that they previously gave to their parents and give it to them instead (see Matthew 15:3-9).

Some leaders have fallen prey to this same self-serving attitude and like the Pharisees try to manipulate teachings in Scripture to benefit themselves. That is why giving offerings must be done prayerfully and not impulsively. When not led by the Holy Spirit, but, inspired by our desire to earn the approval of our leaders, excessive giving can be very harmful. This impulsive, misdirected giving can cause us to become inordinately attached to our leaders and tremendously disappointed by them.

Investing In His Kingdom- Or Man's?

A young couple who had recently joined a small church heard an inspiring sermon about sacrificial giving. Feeling sure that God wanted them to donate towards the small church's building fund, they determined to obey and give all they had. Emptying their savings account of its few thousand dollars, they deposited it in the following week's offering plate. To their dismay, the pastor never acknowledged their sacrifice with even a word of thanks. They had diligently saved their money towards the purchase of a house. Now it was gone, and they concluded that those they gave it to did not appreciate it—or them.

Though it was a costly lesson, they profited from what they learned. From that time forward, each time they attended a service where an inspirational speaker made a request for a large donation, they went home and spent time praying about the matter. Unless they both agreed as a couple, they did nothing. These times of prayer trained them in hearing the voice of the Holy Spirit.

Many years have passed and they have continued to give sacrificially—but never under compulsion and never with regret. During the ensuing years, they gave sacrificially to church building funds, organizations that fed the poor, and helped with offerings for church improvements. Each time they were assured by the Holy Spirit when they were to give and just how much. No matter what the outcome, whether they were appreciated or ignored, they remained cheerful. They were giving to God, not to a man. It is clear by their lives that they put this scripture into practice: *"Remember this: Whoever sows sparingly will also reap sparingly, and whoever sows generously will also reap generously. Each man should give what he has decided in his heart to give, not reluctantly or under compulsion, for God loves a cheerful giver" (2 Corinthians 9:6-7).*

If God was truly sought each time we felt led to give, over and above our tithe, then we would be giving to our King for His kingdom. Keeping our motives pure in this regard is imperative because many people feel terribly taken advantaged of when they give to another out of wrong motives.

This will require that we wait until we are absolutely sure that we have heard from the Lord concerning our desire to donate. Often times an impulsive action is inspired by a charismatic speaker and not by the Holy Spirit. Getting apart with Him and listening for His leading, will afford us the protection of His guidance and assure us of the correct amount He wants us to contribute. Far greater than these benefits, is the assurance that He remains our King. Worshipping Him with our financial gifts is extremely pleasing to Him and, as His word promises, will bring great blessings to us. *"But when you give to the needy, do not let your left hand know what your right hand is doing, so that your giving may be in secret. Then your Father who sees what is done in secret, will reward you" (Matthew 6:3-4).*

Selfless Giving

A wonderful example of selfless giving is powerfully portrayed in John 6:1-13 by an unexpected individual. This inspiring person was a young boy who gave his lunch, five small barley loaves of bread and two small fish, to Jesus with remarkable results. When he heard the Lord ask His disciples to feed the hungry crowd of five thousand, he unselfishly offered his entire lunch to Jesus. Accepting the youngster's generous but meager gift; Jesus blessed it and asked His apostles to distribute the bread and fish to the five thousand hungry people. Astounding everyone present, all were fed until they were satisfied; and the boy was given twelve baskets of leftovers to bring home to his family.

The miraculous multiplication of the loaves and the fish clearly demonstrated that trusting Jesus with the little we have will bring amazing results. The boy with the loaves and the fish gave all he had to Jesus. Because he gave them to Jesus and not to a man or an institution, he got twelve basketfuls in return. That is what happens when we give to Jesus purely because He asks us for all we have — or even a little of what we possess. He multiplies what we give back to us. When we give to men, we will walk away empty handed, unappreciated and will feel taken advantage of for our generosity.

The benefits to serving Jesus far outweigh the benefits of serving man or ourselves. There is no increase, just loss, when we serve anyone other than Jesus.

Imagine if another youth saw the first boy give his lunch to Jesus and then run happily home to his mother with dinner for the entire village. Continue to envisage that he then decided to do the same, so that he would have the same return on the investment of his lunch. Determined to reproduce what he saw happen to his friend, the very next day he gave his lunch to a preacher that was ministering to a crowd. In this imaginary story we are telling, the preacher took the lunch, ate it himself, and shared it with no one because there was only enough for him. Sadly the boy left disappointed and disillusioned, and empty handed, with no return on his sacrificial gift.

This fictitious story is a graphic illustration of what is happening to many in the church today. We hear Scriptures about sacrificial giving and stories of people who give flagrantly to Jesus and walk away with a great return. So in our enthusiasm, we attempt to imitate the gregarious generosity of others and give as well. The problem is that in the giving, we forget the principle doesn't work unless we give our gift to Jesus because He asks us for it and needs the donation for His kingdom. He will always multiply back to us whatever He asks us to give Him. Giving to man for any other reason will only produce disappointment and loss. Our giving must be directed to Jesus, for Jesus, and in obedience to Jesus-as He clearly leads us-and not when under compulsion from another.

The church today has trumpeted the call to give and many have responded with the wrong motives—giving to a man and truly not to Jesus. Under the pretence of giving offerings because we are serving God, many wrong motives can hide: trying to impress the pastor with our generosity, wanting to manipulate the leaders into doing what we want, being accepted by the in-crowd (those sitting on the altar or in the front seats of the church), winning God's approval, being promoted within the church to a position of leadership or into a long desired ministry, receiving the praises of men and the acclaim of a benefactor, or like the youth in our fictitious story, looking for a large return on our gift.

It is not wrong to give. In truth, God commands us to: *"Give, and it will be given to you. A good measure, pressed down, shaken together and running over, will be poured into your lap. For with the measure you use, it will be measured to you" (Luke 6:38).* But many in the church today are giving for the wrong reason, to the wrong people, often when under compulsion, and are receiving no reward. Eventually, this tremendous disappointment leads to a great sense of loss and deprivation. To give all and to walk away empty handed is the fate of many in the church today. Compounding the problem is the reality that in giving to men who are imperfect, many times those benefactors are mistreated instead of appreciated.

Men are frequently prone to sin and for this reason, the Bible says to trust no man. *"Cursed is the one who trusts in man, and depends on flesh for his strength and whose heart turns away from the Lord. He will be like a bush in the wastelands" (Jeremiah 17:5-6).* In the church world, we often forget God's warning, and instead of placing all of our trust in Jesus, we place it in men appointed to lead us. God alone knows what is in the heart of men. He alone can reveal those who He has chosen to receive what He wants us to give. In the Scripture story of the young boy, Jesus directed the child to give the lunch to His disciples, who then passed it out to the crowd. He knows who will pass it out to the crowds and who will heap it on themselves or use it to build their own kingdoms.

Misdirected Giving

Jesus taught, *"The Spirit gives life, the flesh counts for nothing" (John 6:63).*

Those things done out of our flesh, or out of our own desires, profit us nothing. Only those things that are led by the Holy Spirit and done for love of God will bear any fruit in our lives and in the lives of those who surround us.

For this reason, it is essential to go to Jesus for direction in our giving. Never presume; but always pray and receive His direction. Our giving can benefit God and His kingdom and give us a great reward; or it can benefit men, build their kingdom and cause us to lose all. The losses we incur with this kind of unselfish, sacrificial service to the wrong people or the wrong ideologies are many.

The first one noted is the loss of one's self-respect and confidence in dealing with matters of faith and finances. An incredible feeling of worthlessness has enveloped many who, after giving selflessly, were met with ingratitude and poverty. This has been revealed to me firsthand by some much wounded individuals who have recounted their experiences of financial abuse.

A few reported that after taking out loans or re-mortgaging their homes at the request of their pastors for building funds, they found themselves deeply in debt. Their apparent inability to judge these financial matters, under the pressure exerted from their pastors, so impacted their lives that they lost the reliance in their capability to make sound decisions. Feeling disappointed that a man of God had led them to make a decision that so adversely affected their families devastated them, ruined their self-esteem, and shook their faith. A few people confronted the minister to whom they gave the large offering and were turned away without receiving any help or refund. To make the matter worse, they were shunned and kept from attending the church they previously supported because they were seen as trouble-makers.

A number of couples related that they were counseled by their pastors that they were in financial hardship because they lacked faith in God. It was pointed out to them that if they truly believed that the Lord would provide for them, they would not be in lack. This level of accusation only served to heap more abuse on the already disheartened people.

Another devastating result of giving for the wrong reason is the fact that many of these hurting individuals no longer attend church or place themselves under the care of a Godly leader. Some meet with a few other like-minded Christians to pray and share the word, making sure that no one is considered the leader. But most of those who were so terribly hurt will not assemble with anyone. Because they have encountered such devastation in their own personnel lives in the name of Christianity, they shun all organized religious services.

The Church-A Place of Healing

Jesus left us the church as one of His greatest gifts. It was initiated for our good. Through the church His people would be instructed in His ways, healed of their diseases, set free from all that oppressed them, empowered to help others, and meet the needs of one another. *"The Lord God said, 'It is not good for (the) man to be alone'" (Genesis 2:18).* In a church atmosphere, we can support one another, thereby, guarding ourselves from deception and pride. Independence offers no such advantages.

With each story that I heard of selfless giving, above the tithe, which resulted in disillusionment, the Holy Spirit led me to instruct these individuals to forgive those who misled them. After they forgave, I told them to picture Jesus standing in front of them. Then I asked them to picture themselves giving the Lord the offering they had donated to the ministry that disappointed them. Almost immediately, as they gave their offering directly to Jesus—in the spirit—they felt a release from the resentment that was destroying their peace.

He sees the tears, and knows the pain of rejection that hides buried in every wounded heart. As I prayed for those rejected ones, the Holy Spirit gave me a word of encouragement for them: *"I have come to heal the broken hearted. If man rejects you, but I accept you and put My stamp of approval on your life, why does sorrow fill your heart? Just continue to guard your heart from bitterness and resent-*

ments gaining entrance. Love all and in the act of loving, a river of healing will flow to you and through you to those in need of that same healing. Love all, even the wicked and ungrateful. Love all with My love and My power that lies within you. Think good thoughts and quickly forgive all—for your hearts sake."

The Principle of Sowing and Reaping

God's kingdom is established on solid principles. The Lord taught some of these principles through parables. One of the stories he told was of a farmer who went out to sow seeds in his garden. In this story the seed that he planted in rich fertile soil produced a large crop: *"But the one who received the seed that fell on good soil is the man who hears the word and understands it. He produces a crop, yielding a hundred, sixty or thirty times what was sown"* *(Matthew 13:23)*. Once we understand His word to us and begin to act upon it, like a farmer who has planted his crop, we will receive the fruit of our labor. By faith in His promises, our deeds done for love of Him will yield an abundance of goodness back to us.

One of the basic principles of His kingdom is that whatever we sow we will surely reap. Scanty sowing produces a meager harvest. A seed sown here and there from field to field brings forth a plant here and a plant there. But seeds sown generously in the fertile soil of a field that is well tended will produce a hearty, healthy harvest both in the natural realm and in the spirit as well.

Every declaration of faith, every act of kindness, every promise believed and stood upon will bear a crop of its own. No deed, no action no matter how insignificant it seemed at the time will be forgotten or cast aside. All deeds done for love of Him will be sown into the rolling pastures of our lives.

A day will come when His angels will be gathering the harvest of our good actions, which they will bring into God's heavenly kingdom. He promises that we will be rewarded for each and every seed sown and all the fruit they bear. Twofold is the reaping that this harvest will bear. The one is in heaven; the other upon the earth. Good deeds will produce good deeds back to us. Love will bring forth love; loyalty and devotion the same. The fruit of faith will bear miracles. Finances sown will bear prosperity, and all that we need will be supplied.

One day the Lord spoke to me about deeds done for love of Him: *"The fainthearted that hold tightly to their gifts and provision and do not sow them back into Me, will not receive the provision their seed was intended to produce in their lives. Tightfisted, they have walked through life, unable to give freely as I direct. Fear of lack has crippled many into inactivity. Give freely and frequently, as I prompt you, and receive the abundant overflow obedient service always* provides. *I am a faithful God who gives to those who give to Mine for love of Me."*

Benefactors Are Born In the Soil of Sacrifice

Think of the lad who gave Jesus his bread and fish. Oh, what a great crop of loaves and fish it produced for him. Running home laden with the fruit of his generosity, eager to share his propitious reward, his generous nature insured him of hunger free days and wealth to continue to share with others. Benefactors are born in the soil of sacrifice. He had to give before he was positioned to receive.

The fragrance that pours out of our good deeds, done for love of Jesus, ascends to His throne room like incense, where it is taken by His angels and poured out upon the earth to entice others into the same devoted service. The good example of many generous individuals inspires others to give wholeheartedly for the love of God.

William's Story

Each of us is given a plot of land—or a life—to sow seeds of loving service into while on the earth. The memory of a wonderful gentleman, I once had the privilege of knowing has never left me. He is now in heaven reaping his great reward from the seeds of love he sowed while living on the earth. His life inspired many to live fully and selflessly for

Jesus. The fragrance of his loving generosity stills lingers on the earth today.

Because he treasured his privacy, I will not disclose his true name but will call him William. Growing up during the Great Depression was the backdrop of his young life. At a very young age his mother died. Desperate for someone to raise his children, William's father asked his wife's sister if she would leave England, come to the United States and marry him so his children would have a mother. This dedicated woman left everything and embraced William and his siblings as her own. The Lord knew exactly what William needed when he gave him this woman of faith for his mother. She instructed him in the ways of the Lord and because of her tender teaching and loving example; William embraced a lively faith in Jesus Christ. His relationship with the Lord became the mighty foundation of his life and the guideline for all the decisions he made.

The Lord smiled upon this boy—or so it appeared. All throughout his childhood he worked, ran errands, and expressed his love for His Master by performing many kind deeds. Living during the Great Depression impacted William dramatically. Seeing others in need filled his young impressionable heart with compassion for the poor. He knew the pain of hunger, yet he freely gave to those less fortunate than he. Whenever possible he found ways to earn a few pennies to help at home or give to a hungry neighbor.

When William reached manhood, he entered the military to serve his God and his nation. After his stint in the service, he returned home and began a small construction company. Little by little it grew. As it did, he gave. Friends and family members were in need. William unobtrusively reached out and helped each one.

A few years later, he married the love of his life. William and his sweet wife brought his mother into their home where she lived until she died. A few years later, his wife's mom needed a home. So William rented a lovely apartment for her, remodeled it and cared for her the remainder of her life.

As the years progressed, he prospered. The seeds of sacrifice were maturing and bearing their fruit. His business flourished. He and his wife, Mary, sang hymns on public radio every week; and the fragrance of his good deeds spread. As time went on, he felt led to invest in the stock market. Touched by the hand of God, all he invested grew. Soon he became a millionaire.

The church needed to be painted. No one told him. He just noticed. So he hired a company to do the work. William called the pastor and told him to expect a crew to paint the outside of the church; and while they were at it, they would paint the inside of the church, too. All this was done behind the scenes. His only stipulation was that no one was to know he paid for the work. Similarly, while attending a service, he noticed the chairs were getting shabby and the carpet worn.

Once again the surprised pastor got a call to expect new padded chairs and the carpeting of his choice.

With the skilled eye of a contractor, William realized that the roof was in dire need of repair. A patch job was not acceptable by William's standards; not for the house of God. While the busy pastor took care of the needs of his parishioners, William took bids on replacing the roof of the tired church. After all was settled, the pastor received another surprise phone call, "Expect a crew to arrive Monday morning to replace the roof of your church." Months later he bought the busy pastor a new van to use to bring the disadvantaged to church.

William knew that without his help the poor church would not be able to survive. The expense of keeping up the old building was far above what the congregation could afford. Never did he look for acclaim for his generosity. Never did he regret giving. Rather, he thoroughly enjoyed lavishing his pastor and the church with these gifts.

Never tiring of his generosity, William was constantly on the look out to see how he could help the needy. His heart's desire was to bring souls into God's kingdom and to let Jesus love the poor through him. Often after a night of prayer, he would be seen plotting his next scheme to bless those the Lord had asked him to assist. A car for a single mom, food for the poor, money orders mailed to unsuspecting individuals: were but a few of the ideas he felt led to implement.

His story would be incomplete without telling how the seeds of love he faithfully sowed into God's kingdom were reaped in his own life. As he and his wife progressed in years, she developed Alzheimer's disease. Unable to care for her on his own, William and Mary went to live together in a nursing home. Because they married late in life, they had no children to care for them. That was about to change.

Unbeknownst to William, the Lord was getting ready to bless him for all he had done for His children. A church group came to visit the patients and sing for them at the nursing home. William and Mary were delighted. The leader of the church outreach group immediately struck up a friend-ship with the loving couple. Within a month William and Mary were invited to go and live with the leader and her husband. They just happened to have an adorable vacant in-law apartment attached to their home. This couple also had ten foster children, two dogs and a cat. William and Mary accepted the invitation and joined the family. What William didn't know when he agreed to join their large family was that the foster parent's greatest desire was for their little children to know the love of grandparents. God graciously answered the couple's secret desire and instantly their family was complete.

William and Mary were known as 'Grandma and Grandpa' the rest of their lives. For seven wonderful years they shared their lives with the couple and their children, during which time they became surrogate grandparents to all the rest of their children—not just the ten at the house. Even William's long wished for dog became a dream come true. One of the families black labs adopted William as his own. The remainder of William's life was spent reaping blessing after blessing for all the seeds he had so diligently sowed into God's kingdom. This unlikely family went on numerous vacations: camping together, a long wished for trip to Florida and many weekend getaways. Never lonely again: nieces, nephews, pets, children, grandchildren, their grateful pastor and many new special friends graced their lives.

They sowed love and generosity into the heart of their God, never expecting to receive anything but satisfaction back. What a tremendous surprise the Lord pour out on them. William and Mary were given their hearts desires because God was more faithful to them than they were to Him. They selflessly took care of their parents in their elder years. So his God made sure that those seeds sown for love of Him reaped a harvest of children caring for them in their twilight years. We can never outdo God in generosity. We might sow one seed of kindness but will reap thirty, sixty, or one hundred-fold back. Remember: *"But the one who received the seed that fell on good soil is the man who hears the word and understands it. He produces a crop, yielding a hundred, sixty or thirty times what was sown" (Matthew13:23).* William heard the word from his adopted mother, understood it and acted upon it. What a wonderful crop her words produced through his life.

Life's Imperfections

There is another chapter in the life of William and Mary that cries to be told. During the last few years of his life, true to his nature, William gave generously to another church he visited. He observed that this large church lacked a baptismal. He called for a meeting with the pastor and gave him a check to pay for this necessity. Perceiving the future expansion of this growing church and its potential to reach the lost for Christ, William and Mary paid for a large balcony to be built and new chairs delivered to fill it. Cameras were needed for their television ministry, so William bought them as well. Two new vans were also donated to bring his favorite—the less fortunate—to church. Always with an eye for the future, this loving couple embraced the vision of the pastor and helped him build a large Christian Academy for the youth in the region with a very generous donation.

Before his death, William fell and broke his hip. After a week in the hospital, he was sent to a local nursing home to recuperate. Other than his immediate family, his adopted family and his long time pastor, very few went to visit him. It is wonderful that William was such a generous man. But it behooves us to never forget that when someone blesses us, we must be there for them when they are in need as well.

Both as members of a congregation and leaders, we are called by Jesus to love first and foremost. The stress and responsibilities of our families, our jobs and our ministries should never interfere with our commission to care for His children. William was faithful to care for multitudes; but those multitudes forgot him when he was hurting.

What a different picture the Lord would have painted on the canvas of his life if we would have let Him. Streams of grateful friends would have been seen visiting William, their arms laden with flowers and candy. The walls of his room decorated with all the colorful get well cards sent by those he had helped. Instead only those very close to him graced that painting of his last days.

"Prejudice Produces Pain!"

"I charge you, in the sight of God and Christ Jesus and the elect angels, to keep these instructions without partiality, and do nothing out of favoritism" *(1 Timothy 5:21).*

"But the wisdom that comes from heaven is first of all pure; then peace-loving, considerate, submissive, full of mercy and good fruit, impartial and sincere" *(James 3:17).*

Chapter Five

Preferential Treatment

One day a sweet, wonderful woman I have grown to love told me her story. She grew up in South America. As a child she regularly attended Sunday service. Because her parents had never married, she was shunned by the local priest. Her memories of attending Mass were of walking up to the priest after the service was over and being pushed aside to make way for the more accepted members to greet him. Her illegitimacy hung around her neck like a sign declaring that she was to be scorned.

A tremendous feeling of worthlessness, especially in regards to her spirituality, settled on her as a result of the continuous rejection by her pastor. It has taken her many years to realize that she is precious to God and acceptable to Him. Now she is a powerful intercessor and walks in intimate fellowship with the Holy Spirit. It is evident to all that know her that God honors her. Her prayers are mighty and effectual just like Scripture declares: *"The prayer of a righteous man is powerful and effective" (James 5:16).* Many have been healed and rescued as a result of her faith filled prayers.

This is not the only story that I have been told of someone being given preferential treatment while others were being rejected. Just recently, it was revealed to a wealthy woman that when she and her family began attending a large church, the leaders were instructed to give them exceptional attention. It was the custom of that church to make everyone feel welcome. But this couple, because of their outstanding social standing, was to be sought after. She was offended that the kind treatment she received had ulterior motives behind it. The realization that what she could give the church mattered more than whom she was, offended her deeply. That attitude was one she and her husband dealt with in the business world. This experience made them feel like the church was being run like a corporation. In their eyes, it no longer resembled a house of prayer, nor a place the wounded could come for help. They went there looking for Jesus, seeking the help He could give their family, and left disillusioned.

At the same time, a disadvantaged family was attending this identical church. Every Sunday this single mom was picked up from the inner-city where they lived and brought to the service by the church's van ministry. She and her five children attended church faithfully. After many months it was decided that those using the van were to pay a few dollars per person both ways. Because her family was so large and her income very limited, she could not afford to ride the van. All the teachings she faithfully listened to each Sunday now lost their impact. What was happening to her did not coincide with the Word of God she heard and read. *"And do not forget to do good and share with others, for with such sacrifices God is pleased" (Hebrews 13:16).* And: *"He who gives to the poor will lack nothing, but he who closes his eyes to them receives many curses" (Proverbs 28:27).* Disappointed and heartbroken, this family left the church and found one near their home where they were accepted, given the assistance they needed, and treated like everyone else.

The Holy Spirit knows our natural tendency to be self-seeking so He warns us in James: *"My brothers, as believers in our glorious Lord Jesus Christ, don't show favoritism. Suppose a man comes into your meeting wearing a gold ring and fine clothes, and a poor man in shabby clothes also comes in. If you show special attention to the man wearing fine clothes and say, 'Here's a good seat for you,' but say to the poor man, 'You stand there' or 'Sit on the floor by my feet,' have you not discriminated among yourselves and become judges with evil thoughts" (James 2:1-4)?*

Imagine how wonderful our churches would be if we would obey the dictates in this Scripture. People who could not afford clothing for church would not stay home for fear of being rejected or judged. All would be given the same opportunities to minister in God's house regardless of their financial status or level of education. The Holy Spirit would have free reign to promote people in His kingdom and delegate authority to whomever He wanted. Everyone would feel accepted regardless of their past mistakes. This is the atmosphere of heaven: love, acceptance, worthiness, joy, unity. Jesus instituted His church to prepare us for heaven and give us a foretaste of the glory that resides there. Each of us should leave church experiencing a glimpse of the wonders that our Father has prepared for us.

It is not God's plan for us to go to church and find ourselves being cast aside for someone more worthy. Nor is it meant to be a place where we are judged and found wanting because of our social standing or level of income. Neither should it ever be a place where we are sought after for our gifts, talents or resources to advance the church's ministries. Church should be a refuge from the competition and chaos that we encounter in our daily lives.

Self-serving Attitudes Breed Destruction

A church on the West Coast of the United States was building a large addition to their facility. The plumbing had to be updated and the going rate beyond what they wanted to spend. To the great delight of the overburdened pastor, a young couple had recently joined the church and he just happened to own a plumbing business. Tom and Marie were newlyweds. Marie had just given birth to their son. Life for them was full of adjustments and many pressures. The level of stress increased on this couple as they encountered all the difficulties of managing their new family and the financial pressure of running a business escalated. During this adjustment period, the pastor of the church approached Tom and asked if he would volunteer to install their new plumbing system.

Inspiring the church members to work at the church evenings and Saturdays was the focus of many of the pastor's sermons. Everyone was taught that serving God in this capacity would be a pleasing sacrifice that God would reward. Those who did not commit totally were depicted as lacking in diligence and spiritually weak. Feeling a tremendous responsibility to serve God and the church in this capacity, and ashamed not to give of his time and talents, led Tom to make a very radical decision.

Tom felt it was his duty to help the men and women of this busy church with the construction effort. So every night after work, he showed up at the church. Without fail Tom could be found working diligently on the plumbing until almost 11:00 PM Mondays through Fridays and all day Saturdays, too.

Meanwhile, Marie was left home alone with her newborn son. Tension and depression showed up at their doorstep, entered the house and never left. No matter how Marie begged Tom to stay home with his family, he refused because he had given his word to complete the project at the church. Weeks turned into months and tension developed into deep resentment. A gulf developed between Tom and Marie that eventually destroyed their marriage.

Wrapped up in the pressure of getting the building project completed, the pastor did not advise Tom that leaving his new family every night was not wise. If the Holy Spirit was consulted, I'm sure that He would have counseled the pastor and Tom with a much better way to get the plumbing accomplished without destroying the tender relationship between Tom and Marie. Scripture is clear about such matters: *"Finally, all of you, live in harmony with one another; be sympathetic, love as brothers, be compassionate and humble" (1 Peter 3:8).*

A great tragedy resulted and this family was destroyed. Though they saved the church a large sum of money, the price Tom and Marie paid was exorbitant.

The Price of Compassion

A friend of mine approached me with a compassionate plea. She had just returned from a trip to Austria. In the past, we had visited that country together and prayed for many people while there. Because of our reputation as missionaries, a young mother went to see her.

Stella was desperate. She was a single mother raising her four year old son herself, and she had been diagnosed with cancer. The cancer had not responded to treatment; and the doctor told her he could not help her any further. She was instructed to come back when her lungs filled up with fluid. At that time he would attempt to drain them, but that was all he could do for her.

Weeks before my friend arrived in Austria, Stella contacted a priest for prayers for God to heal her. The minister told her he would be pleased to pray for her, after she paid him $2000.00. Stella did not have the money to pay for his prayers. While telling her story to a friend, she was informed of our ministry. As soon as my friend arrived in Austria, Stella was at her home begging her to have our ministry pray for her.

Once my missionary friend told me Stella's sad story, we set on a course of action. We decided to pray for Stella long distance, from New England to Austria, every week on the phone. I will never forget that first phone contact. Stella offered to pay us what she could, but explained that her means were limited. Immediately, we explained that we never required anyone to pay us for prayer. We told her that it would be our great privilege to pray for Jesus to heal her.

Each week the Holy Spirit led our prayers. One week she accepted Jesus as her Lord and Savior. Another week, she was led to forgive everyone who hurt her. Gradually, she began to see some improvement in her health. She wrote down Scriptures we dictated to her and posted them all about her house. All through the week preceding her prayer with us, she recited those Biblical promises. Daily her faith grew. Finally, one very eventful Saturday afternoon, while we prayed on the phone from the USA to Europe, the power of God fell on this young, desperate mother. In a vision, I saw her spine glowing like molten lava. Obeying what I observed in this graphic vision, I prayed for the fire of God to fall on her and consume the cancer. That is exactly what happened. She began to scream that she was on fire. She ran through her house opening the windows because she could not stand the intensity of the heat that fell on her. I explained through my friend, who interpreted our conversations that God was healing her and sometimes it feels like a mighty fire. We laughed and thanked Jesus. A few weeks later, at her next appointment with her doctor, they could find no cancer. All the tumors had disappeared.

This happened a few years ago and she is completely healed to this day. Not only did God heal her body, but He restored her relationships with her father and her son's father. And God did it all for free! He is no respecter of persons. He doesn't play favorites or give preferential treatment to a few. All who come to His throne of grace and mercy can receive His blessings free of charge.

Unity and Equality

Before Jesus left the Passover feast to begin His work of paying the price for our sins, He prayed an unforgettable prayer. This conversation with His Father revealed His passion for unity. *"My prayer is not for them alone. I pray also for those who will believe in me through their message, that all of them may be one, Father, just as you are in me and I am in you...May they be brought to complete unity to let the world know that you sent me and have loved them even as you have loved me" (John 17:20-21,23).* He prayed that we would be brought to total and complete unity with one another and with Him. Without this unity, we will not accomplish the work of saving the lost. If the world looks at us and sees competition, jealousy, preferential treatment to a few while others are ignored; they will not be attracted to His kingdom.

It will look no different to them than the place where they reside in the world. When people are led to make a change, it is always because they perceive a benefit will come from it. What would the benefit be to leave the pursuit of the pleasures of this world in exchange for the pursuit of the vanities we have brought into the church? Jockeying for positions of authority, struggling to live in harmony in our families amidst the untoward stress of additional responsibilities at church, trying to make ends meet while others are undermining these efforts by their excessive demands will not attract but will repel those looking for a change in their lives.

Unless we truly follow Jesus and give up all fleshly desires for prominence and fame, we will just bring the miseries of the world into the church. Jealousy will stifle the spiritual growth and undermine the quest for holiness of the Body of Christ. Instead, the church must be a healthy haven where its members are tucked away from the competition and chaos of the world.

Overwhelmed
By
Control!"

"We ought therefore to show hospitality to such men so that we may work together for the truth.

I wrote to the church, but Diotrephes, who loves to be first, will have nothing to do with us. Not satisfied with that, he refuses to welcome the brothers. He also stops those who want to do so and puts them out of the church.

Dear friend, do not imitate what is evil but what is good"
(3 John 8-11).

"And let us consider how we may spur one another on toward love and good deeds. Let us not give up meeting together, as some are in the habit of doing, but let us encourage one another—" (Hebrews 10:24-25).

Chapter Six

Overstepping Boundaries

A fter much research, a young couple who recently moved to a suburb outside of Chicago joined a church in their neighborhood. The church appeared to have every-thing they were looking for: A Spirit filled worship service laced with friendly church members. Inspirational messages every Sunday and a Christian school for their three children to attend.

Embracing the church as an extended family, they quickly made their presence felt. Bob became an elder and usher, while Nancy helped watch the babies in the nursery and offered her services with secretarial work. Always a gracious homemaker, Nancy opened her home to the kind people they accepted as their friends. Dinner parties, fellow-ships after church, craft meetings were but a few of the events they wholeheartedly hosted. As the years passed their bonds of friendship grew with the members of their church family.

Eager to raise their children in the Christian faith, they enrolled all three of them in the grammar school attached to the church. As is the custom in many private Christian schools, the children wore uniforms. One Sunday the two boys went to church in their uniforms, as was required, but one of the boys forgot to wear his belt. When he arrived at school on Monday morning, their son was given detention for not being in complete uniform at church. Both Bob and Nancy felt this was unreasonable. They fully accepted the policy that the children were to wear their complete uniforms to school but felt their role as parents was being usurped. The rule of requiring the children to wear their uniforms on Sundays felt intrusive of their rights. They preferred to have their children dress the way they wanted them to when not attending school. After thinking the situation through, they decided to ignore it.

Even more concerning was the corporal punishment the children were receiving for misbehavior during school. It was the policy of the school to use spanking to control certain behaviors. This too greatly bothered Bob and Nancy. They believed it was their responsibility to discipline their children—not the school's.

A few weeks after these events surfaced, Nancy was fulfilling her responsibility to watch the babies in the nursery. Bob was also scheduled to usher during that service. In order to make sure that their three children were behaving, they asked a friend if one of the boys could sit with him while

Bob ushered. All was going smoothly until a deacon spotted little Billy not sitting with his parents. The deacon curtly chastened Billy and told him to go sit with his parents. Even though the situation was carefully explained, the deacon insisted that the child could not sit with anyone but his parents. Billy was removed from his seat and sat alone until Bob was finished ushering.

Very upset at the way they and their son were treated, they made an appointment to speak with the pastor. Fully understanding that the church had a policy that children must sit with their parents, they thought that once the situation was explained, the pastor would correct the mishandling of their son. Instead, the pastor insisted that there was no allowance for parents who were engaged in ministry to have someone else watch their children during the service. The meeting ended with both sides in direct disagreement. No compromise was struck. The heart of the pastor was revealed to Bob and Nancy and the level of his control evident.

They had listened to many sermons on the importance of submission to the authority of the pastor. Their pastor had frequently quoted, *"Obey your leaders and submit to their authority. They keep watch over you as men who must give an account. Obey them so that their work will be a joy, not a burden, for that would be of no advantage to you" (Hebrews 13:17).* Bob and Nancy thoroughly understood the position of leadership that their pastor held. They had no problem submitting to his directives; but it appeared that he was overstepping his bounds of authority. When his decisions directly affected their rights to parent their own children, they knew they must take a stand. Their responsibility to raise their children the way God was leading them to parent them, superseded the pastors right to govern the church and the school.

Knowing they could not in good conscience allow this abuse of their authority as parents continue, they made the difficult decision to leave the church and remove their children from the school. Just as when Paul told the church: *"We are not trying to please men but God, who tests our hearts" (1 Thessalonians 2:4);* they knew that their responsibility was not to please the pastor, but to do what pleased God.

Little did they realize the level of control that this pastor dictated. A few days after officially leaving the church, Nancy had a visitor. Her close friend who was helping her sew drapes for her living room came to see her. She explained that once they finished sewing Nancy's drapes, she would no longer be able to speak with her. The pastor had issued a directive to the church that Bob, Nancy and their three children were in rebellion and were to be shunned by the entire church.

No one ever reached out to this hurting family. They lost all their friends. The phone stopped ringing. The fellowships at their home were never to be again. Even the casual craft meetings were halted. All of the children's playmates disappeared. No more bike rides together, football games, or excursions to the mall. A huge void now existed in their lives and in their hearts. This discipline was purposely intended to bring them the pain that it did. Because they disagreed with the pastor and left the church, this was their punishment.

Nowhere in scripture does God direct anyone to abuse others for any reason—and never because they disagree with us. Jesus came to teach us a better way: the way of love and forgiveness. When someone takes a Scripture and bases his philosophy on it without taking the full spirit of the gospel into account, great harm can result. Yes, we are supposed to obey and honor our leaders. We are also supposed to use our heads and recognize when someone is overstepping their bounds of authority and infringing on our rights.

Recovery A Long Slow Process

It took many years for this family to recover from the abuse they suffered when a leader tried to usurp their authority and call it his own. Heartbroken, they gradually made new friends and found a new church to attend. It took many years for them to trust another leader and feel like a member of a church family again. Sadly, Bob and Nancy's three children suffered the most from the abuse and rejection of this church. In the name of Jesus Christ, they were mistreated. Now, as adults, they have made the decision to forego church attendance. The hypocrisy they encountered is still engrained in their hearts. In their young impressionable minds, Christ was depicted as an unreasonable tyrant. How could they ever desire to embrace a tyrant as their friend?

Through the years as they attended other churches with their parents, these three children saw those same qualities of control and abuse in other leaders. If they had met sincere, holy leaders, I'm sure they would have seen the heart of Christ and fallen in love with Him.

Susan's Story

The travesty that was done to this family is not uncommon. Frequently, I have heard similar stories. Sitting over lunch with a group of friends, the beautiful, soft spoken, middle-aged woman sitting opposite me began to relate a very painful memory.

Susan was married to her childhood sweetheart while just a teenager. During her twenty years of marriage, her husband had become a terrible tyrant. Fear ruled her life. Never knowing what would upset her abusive, volatile husband, she learned to manage her four children and her household as carefully as possible.

The stress of living with a man who continually emotionally abused her became unbearable for Susan. She contemplated ending her life. Thankfully, her sister talked her out of it. Susan sought marriage counseling instead. Nothing changed. The abuse continued and her despair deepened.

During most of their married life, Susan and her husband attended an independent church. They and their four children were very active members there. To the common observer all looked well. Their four children even went to the Christian academy sponsored by the church.

One year later, after resisting the desire to end her life and after seeking counseling, Susan was still terribly unhappy. With no other options available, she decided to leave her tyrannical husband. Because of their financial situation and the controlling influence of her demanding husband on their children, Susan's four children were going to stay in their home with him.

When the one of the elders of their church heard that she was leaving her husband, he called her. The depth of the lack of compassion expressed by this church official is etched in her memory as if it happened yesterday. He explained that the Bible teaches that she could not get a divorce and leave her husband and family. Instead, she was to reconcile and submit to her husband. She explained that his abusive treatment was unbearable, and she could not continue to live that way. His response was that the church would not continue to stand beside her if she persisted in her plan to leave. She was considered in rebellion to the teachings in Scripture and to her leaders, by divorcing her husband.

Susan knew it was a matter of life or death for her. She could not bear the continuous abuse any longer. Despite the rebuff by the church, she left. For many months, Susan slept every night cowering in her closet with the door closed tightly. Shunned by her church family, no longer able to receive the loving attention of her children; fear and sorrow became her only companions.

But, God is good. When the church fails His children, He doesn't. Little by little, He healed and restored Susan's broken life. He brought good, strong friends alongside her, helped her to get a good job and eventually restored her relationship with three of her children.

Susan related to me that the entire situation was tremendously painful, but being shunned by her church family made her lonely life almost unbearable. Their rejection and total lack of emotional and spiritual support brought an avalanche of undeserved guilt into her heart. This guilt over her decision to leave her husband almost paralyzed her and affected her children as well.

While we spoke, I remembered a similar circumstance I had experienced when counseling another friend. She, too, had lived with a very abusive husband and had decided to leave him. Because she was afraid that I would disagree with her decision and try to talk her out of it, she was reluctant to tell me she was leaving. Sitting with Susan, I remembered what the Holy Spirit had place in my heart to tell my other friend in my kitchen many years ago. I explained that the Holy Spirit wanted her to know that *Jesus loved **her**—much more than He hated divorce.* As I related these impacting words that God spoke to my heart many years ago to Susan, her beautiful eyes filled with tears and the guilt she secretly carried in her heart disappeared. Now she knew and understood that her God loved her so much that He did not want her to suffer abuse from anyone in order to satisfy a law — even if it was a good law.

Reflecting the True Heart of Jesus

As representatives of Jesus Christ, leaders are supposed to show their congregants the character of Jesus. When what some leaders reveal is so pain-filled, how can we wonder that many shy away from the church? They have experienced it as a place where you are told what to do, how to do it and shunned if they disagree.

In the past, it was brought to my attention that mature adults were asked to leave their church because the leaders disagreed with personal decisions they were making. Some had expressed a desire to marry and the leaders felt it was unwise. The couples persisted in their request to marry or were married elsewhere. In all cases, they were expelled from the church. To give wise council is the responsibility of the pastors. But to demand that their advice be followed, even when it isn't a matter within the realm of the pastor's responsibility, is over stepping the bounds of a pastor's authority. God has His plans for each man's life. To influence someone's life with our opinions is dangerous and far more controlling than God ordains.

Nowhere in scripture is Jesus revealed as anything but loving, forgiving and understanding. Even though He was the Son of God, He was never abusive nor did He ever overstep His authority.

One day Jesus was able to demonstrate this quality: *"Someone in the crowd said to him, 'Teacher, tell my brother to divide the inheritance with me.' Jesus replied, 'Man, who appointed me a judge or an arbiter between you?'"* *(Luke 12:13-14)*. Everything Jesus did spoke of wisdom, respect and fairness. Love motivated His every word and action.

How different our churches would be if we truly followed Christ's humble example. Women experiencing abuse would be able to receive Godly council and support instead of judgmental demands that could prove to be disastrous. Children would be safe from overbearing, unreasonable elders. In place of feeling rejected and unworthy, they would all feel accepted and cherished. Parents would know that their little ones were being given the proper example of how a truly committed Christian behaves. Dialog would always be open to avoid misunderstanding and keep offenses from simmering within the hearts of those who have been hurt. Leaders would allow differing opinions to be expressed without retaliation even if the decision were made to leave their church. Humility would be the earmark of the church and pride would find no place within its walls. The rights and responsibilities of all: wives, husbands, parents and children would be respected and never thwarted. An atmosphere of mutual consideration and understanding would be fostered and disrespect nonexistent.

In this safe environment, everyone would be equipped to go out and impact the world with the love of Jesus. Scripture exhorts us: *"And let us consider how we may spur one another on toward love and good deeds. Let us not give up meeting together, as some are in the habit of doing, but let us encourage one another—" (Hebrews 10:24-25).*

"Damaged
By
Sexual Abuse!"

"But among you there must not be even a hint of sexual immorality, or of any kind of impurity, or of greed, because these are improper for God's holy people. Nor should there be obscenity, foolish talk or coarse joking, which are out of place, but rather thanksgiving. For of this you can be sure: No immoral, impure or greedy person—such a man is an idolater—has any inheritance in the kingdom of Christ and of God" (Ephesians 5:3-5).

"Finally, be strong in the Lord and in his mighty power. Put on the full armor of God so that you can take your stand against the devil's schemes.... Therefore put on the full armor of God, so that when the day of evil comes, you may be able to stand your ground, and after you have done everything, to stand" (Ephesians 6:10-11,13).

Chapter Seven

The Downfall of Great Leaders

One sunny afternoon, a woman visiting our church from a northern city bared her heart to me. The tragic story she related had happened to her personally and had adversely impacted many of her friends. She asked me to relate it to my readers, perhaps saving others from a similar heartbreak.

She had been a member of a very large congregation. The pastor of her church was in charge of the district churches in their denomination. He was very well known and highly respected. His gift for preaching drew many into his blooming church. This pastor sat on a pedestal of fame and popularity and was considered above reproach.

One day a woman reported that this charismatic pastor had molested her and drawn her into a sexual relationship. She was a single mom and was going through a time of great difficulty in her life. During her counseling appointments with him, she reported that he took advantage of her. He denied the charges.

Because the church and its leaders believed that he could do no wrong, when these accusations surfaced against him, they were immediately discounted. After all, they surmised, this woman's reputation could not compare with his. The leaders were all on his side and vehemently defended him. Deeply committed to him and finding invaluable the prestigious success he brought to the church, they did not want to lose their charismatic leader. They were convinced that dismissing him would cause the demise of the rapidly growing church.

The young woman left the church deeply wounded and in despair. A few months later, unable to cope with the abuse, the injustice and the rejection which followed, she committed suicide.

Many months passed by and then two other women surfaced with similar stories. They, too, had been in difficult situations. Their lives were unstable and their marriages in ruins. They reported that like the first young woman, this pastor had taken advantage of them during their counseling sessions and molested them as well.

This time the board of directors of the church acted. They brought the pastor before them and corrected him for his sexual impropriety. He admitted his indiscretions, apologized and promised he would never commit these transgressions again. After this disciplinary meeting, he was immediately reinstated as acting pastor. Moreover, his devoted wife went into shock when she learned what he had done. The congregation was split. Some stood steadfastly behind him and believed he was being falsely accused, while others believed the women and wanted him deposed.

Months—and eventually years—of unrest followed, when the unthinkable happened. Two more women came forward with reports of his sexual advances. Their accusations of sexual molestation finally found an ear. One of the women that came forward wrote letters to the district council stating exactly what the pastor had done to her. Her expository letters caused them to take action.

This time the pastor, amid the cries of disbelief from the congregants, was deposed. The leaders who replaced him addressed the congregation revealing the 'truth' about the current accusations. In their statement, they inaccurately implied that the women he molested were also to blame for the sexual impropriety of the pastor. One grave injustice to these victims followed another. Abused and falsely accused, they sought help and council outside their church. Soon after this meeting, the unseated pastor was sent away for treatment, while the church continued to pay his salary.

The Collateral Damage of Sexual Abuse

Besides the women he deeply wounded, there were many other victims of this pastor's sexual abuse. His wife and family were scarred by his actions and humiliated by his unfaithfulness to them. He was not just their husband and father but their revered spiritual leader as well. All the years of instruction, especially in regards to holiness and morality, fell into a sinkhole of hypocrisy.

Devastated by the sordid revelations of sexual misconduct by their pastor, the entire membership of the large congregation was left completely disillusioned. Their faith was severely tested. Furthermore, all that they had been taught by him had to be reevaluated. What was the truth and what was just a man's interpretation of that truth? Many researched the Scriptures themselves, while others sought council from other clergy. Those who laid their foundation on Christ recovered quickly. But tragically, those who had built their faith on the pastor took much longer to recuperate. Thankfully, many of the wounded members of this floundering fellowship found solace in good wholesome churches. But to this day, few of the original members of that once thriving church remain within its walls.

The young woman who related this tragic experience was never the same. She became hyper-vigilant about the care of her children. Because of this devastating disappointment, she lost all trust in mankind and would never leave any of her four youngsters with another adult to baby-sit them. No matter where she went, she kept them with her. She surmised that if a man who represented Christ to so many had done the unthinkable, then how could she ever trust anyone with her precious little ones? Suspicion and fear gripped her life and forever changed her.

After months of prayer and extensive searching, she and her husband found a new church to attend. Caution ruled their entrance into this new environment. They held the clergy and the leaders under high scrutiny. Because they had been deceived into trusting their former pastor and his board of directors, they felt insecure in their ability to discern if all was as it appeared to be. Gradually, she and her family began to feel safe in their new house of worship. The love and nurturing environment of this fellowship eventually destroyed their reluctance to connect. Sitting under good solid teaching and allowing God's presence to touch them during worship, helped their hearts to heal. But my friend related that her trust in others was never completely restored.

Secrets Revealed Too Late

A dejected woman confided in her close friend and told her a very tragic story. The tale she disclosed would have shocked anyone who heard it twenty years ago. But sadly to say, the events she related are common today—one our society has become all too accustomed to hearing.

Weeping, pouring her heart out in total dismay, she began to relate this story: The pastor of her church had recently passed away. He just dropped dead while walking in his back yard. This man was a powerful leader and an anointed preacher. Greatly beloved and highly respected by his followers, the entire church went into mourning over their tragic loss.

Soon after his sudden death, several young men came forward with their tales of horror. This trusted leader, who had just died suddenly, had molested them when they were teenagers under his care in the church. Disbelief stung everyone, until the pastor's son, moved by the desire to defend these young men, came forward and recounted the same story. He explained to his grief stricken mother that the stories about his dad were true, because he, too, had been a victim of his father's perversion.

Holding onto the elevated memory of her husband, this unconvinced woman disowned her son. Not only had this young man been abused by his father, but he had been forced to keep his awful experiences of molestation a secret for many years. Now once the truth was revealed, he was completely rejected by his mother and cast away from those closest to him. The damage done to him by his abusive father and angry mother was beyond repair—or so it appeared.

Years have passed since these events unfolded. The once angry, skeptical mother reconciled with her badly wounded son. The Lord was faithful to them both. Through their obedience to forgive, the Lord healed them of many of the deep scars this terrible abuse had brought into their lives.

A Mindset That Aides Abuse

The pastor's wife in the story above is not uncommon in her inability to believe that her husband and pastor could commit such a terrible sin against her son and the young boys in their church. A waitress in a restaurant we frequent heard of my book and began to relate a similar but even more devastating incident.

About ten years ago, a young boy she knew was attending a church in New York with his mother and siblings. He complained to his mom that the minister was sexually molesting him; but his mother did not believe his story. Each time they prepared to go to church, he would tell the same story and beg her not to make him go. Because of her relationship to the pastor and the rest of the members of her church, she refused to believe what her son was saying could possibly be true. She thought it was just his way of getting out of going to church and the other activities he was active in at the church. Therefore, this sexual abuse went on for many years unaltered. The boy—now a young man— suffered enormous damage both from the sexual abuse of his pastor and from the neglect of his mother.

Not only was this family devastated by the effects of the sexual sins of this leader, but those who knew this family were tremendously impacted as well. Our friendly waitress never allowed her children to be alone with anyone—especially a member of the clergy. Disastrous was the level of mistrust, anger and accompanying unbelief that she expressed as she related this painful account. She explained that once the true facts were revealed about the misconduct of this minister, those on the outer fringes of this tragedy stayed away from attending church—not just the church that the offending priest led.

Learning from Other's Misfortunes

These heartrending events will be of no benefit for us to recount or read unless we are taught something from them. Should we learn to trust no man-ever? Should we hide from close relationships, especially in a church setting, as some have? Or should we run a background check on those we are looking to for spiritual guidance? Some of these ideas appear ridiculous, but the reality is that many have developed mindsets aligning with these exaggerated ideas.

When we give any person the place of supremacy in our lives that belongs to God alone, we will always be disillusioned. Thinking a person is infallible and perfect in all their ways is a dangerous and deceptive position. Undoubtedly, they will fail us and never meet our grandiose expectations. Furthermore, this erroneous philosophy blinds those who embrace this mindset to the faults of those so honored. From this dangerous vantage point of impaired vision, sexual abuse often occurs.

As has been related by those who have fallen prey to sexual abusers, they were completely unaware of any problem the perpetrator had and held the person in high regard. The smoke screen of infallibility hid these flaws—along with the potential for abuse—from their view. Completely trusting and void of all suspicion, many were tricked into compromising situations. The trap, set by the demands for excessive adulation and honor, was set. This snare captured many innocent victims; who then experienced the horrors of being molested by a loved and trusted caregiver.

To avoid similar situations, it is imperative that we relegate our care and our adoration to none but our Lord and Savior. Scripture admonishes: *"...in quietness and trust is your strength" (Isaiah 30:15).* His word encourages us to trust Him and receive our strength—not from our leaders—but from Him alone. We will receive peace, protection, guidance and quietness of soul as we lean totally on Him.

When we place our full hope in Him, He will be able to safely use others to train and council us. Once that help is received, then we could appreciate the efforts of those God chooses to use to bless us without endangering ourselves by worshipping them.

Looking to the Lord for help, because we know that He alone is our source, will afford us divine protection. If our eyes are fixed on Him, then we won't place anyone on His throne in our hearts. If the influential person in our lives preached with a tremendous anointing and was effective as a charismatic leader, but began to approach us or others in an inappropriate way, we would not be held captive by their deception. The imperfect would have no ability to hide behind the cloak of feigned perfection and would be denied access into our lives.

When leaders fall away from God's plan and become abusers, the Lord will warn us. The Holy Spirit will lead us away from these leaders, if He is on the throne in our lives. If our spiritual leaders have replaced Him, and the Lord no longer occupies the high place in our lives, then we will be immune to His warnings. If another has our attention, then our ears will be deaf to His voice. His Word reminds us, *"Be still, and know that I am God" (Psalm 46:10).* Let us be still before Him and listen to His voice. He will drown out the voices of confusion and deception and most assuredly position us for His best: Godly leaders, protection from perpetrators, help in our time of need.

Those in leadership positions would do well to learn from those who have fallen into this terrible trap of sexual misconduct. *"There is no difference, for all have sinned and fall short of the glory of God..." (Romans 3:22-23).* Keeping ourselves safe from the temptations that pride offers to those who are respected and revered is essential. Humility will always act as a shield to guard those holding leadership positions from the pitfall of pride that precedes every sin. To frequently acknowledge, in agreement with Scripture, *"... there is no one who does good" (Psalm 14:1)* and: *"There is only One who is good" (Matthew 19:17)* will wash leaders' minds from the stain of self exaltation.

Renewing one's mind daily with the truth of who we are and who God is, as related in the Word of God, is essential. Fully acknowledging that apart from God we can do no good thing, would be just one of the fruits of this practice. In order to help those He has placed under their care, leaders must stay close to the Holy Spirit and far from all that would tempt them away into sin. Cloaked in humility—totally dependent on the righteousness of Christ and not their own righteousness—will insure them of His continual help. Keeping ones flesh subject to the reign of God and not allowing it to run freely, wreaking havoc on innocent victims would be the result of this continual fellowship with the Holy Spirit.

If a weakness or temptation is becoming problematic and difficult to resist, then it is essential to humbly seek help from a trusted Christian leader. Jesus came to set the captives free and to destroy the works of the devil. His children must reap the benefits He so painfully purchased for them. Deliverance is the benefit of being one of His children. For leaders to accept help overcoming a weakness shows great strength of character. True humility, a total dependence on our Savior, and faith in the power of His blood will destroy the yoke of lust and perversion.

David, the great warrior King of Israel, portrays an example in Scripture of one who fell headlong into this pernicious trap of power, pride and lust. A study of his life would greatly help us all—and most especially those who are in positions of leadership. His fall into catastrophic sins serves as a warning, as much as his subsequent contrition and depth of humility, serves as an inspiration.

Destroyed By Lust

Power corrupts. King David, though a man with a heart after God, feel prey to the corrupting influence of power, pride and lust. Before his downfall, David led Israel for many years with great humility and compassion. After a pure-hearted, sincere launching into ministry, some leaders—like David—eventually find themselves snared in the very trap they vehemently opposed years earlier. Sadly, the story of King David's life and the grave mistakes of his later years have been duplicated in the lives of many great leaders.

David was called as a teenager to be the second king of Israel. As the story of his life unfolds, Samuel the prophet was sent by God to Jesse's home to anoint the new king. From Jesse's eight sons God chose the youngest. *"He was ruddy, with a fine appearance and handsome features" (1 Samuel 16:12)*. Though he was good looking, that was not why he was chosen. The Lord explained to Samuel, *"'The Lord does not look at the things man looks at. Man looks at the outward appearance, but the Lord looks at the heart'" (1 Samuel 16:7)*. God approved of the character that David had developed. He had what it took to lead God's people.

Tending his father's herd of sheep had taught him some of the valuable lessons that he needed in order for him to fulfill his destiny as king. Day after day he spent long hours alone on neighboring hillsides grazing the flock. In his own words he explained: *"When a lion or a bear came and carried off a sheep from the flock, I went after it and rescued the sheep from its mouth. When it turned on me, I seized it by its hair, struck it and killed it" (1 Samuel 17:34-35).* The fact that he was strong and valiant, as well as a great protector of those assigned to his care, was not the only reason he caught God's attention. In the chest of this youngster, beat a heart of humility. After slaying the predators of his father's sheep, he declared: *"The Lord who delivered me from the paw of the lion and the paw of the bear will deliver me from the hand of this Philistine" (1 Samuel 17:37).* He didn't boast or brag about his accomplishments but gave the credit for his victories to the Lord. He knew that God was the strength of his life.

While watching the sheep alone under the starry sky, he wrote and sang songs to his God. Reading the psalms he composed, reveals the intense love relationship he developed with the Lord. *"Your love, O Lord, reaches to the heavens; your faithfulness to the skies...How priceless is your unfailing love! Both high and low among men find refuge in the shadow of your wings" (Psalm 36:5, 7).*

It is no wonder that God singled him out to be the next king. His credentials were impeccable. Years after the call to be king was delivered through Samuel, the prophet, and after the death of King Saul, David assumed the throne. All Israel rejoiced in their new king. They believed that this young man had what it took to be their leader.

For many years David did just that. He led his warriors to battle victoriously against their enemies, cared for the poor and destitute in the land, and inspired the people to maintain a pure passionate love for God. Obedience to his God was of paramount concern in his life. In the early years of his reign, no matter what the situation before him, David sought the Lord for guidance. God truly was his strength and source.

Eventually, after many years of reigning under the favor of God, all the power and prestige of being the renowned king of Israel went to David's head. Pride was setting its trap for the unsuspecting king. One fateful evening while his army was out to war, David stayed behind. While strolling on the roof of his palace, he saw Bathsheba, a very beautiful woman bathing. *"Then David sent messengers to get her. She came to him, and he slept with her...Then she went back home. The woman conceived and sent word to David, saying, 'I am pregnant'" (2 Samuel 11:4-5).* Then the catastrophic cover-up began.

The Cover-up Backfires

Immediately, David sent for Bathsheba's husband, Uriah—a mighty warrior in his army—to return from battle.

He initiated this scheme so that Uriah would spend the night with his wife and become the presumed father of her illegitimate child. But the strategy did not unfold as David planned. Uriah was a man of great character. He would not eat, drink and nor go lay with his wife while the army of Israel was camped in open fields. Instead, he slept outside the entrance to the palace with all his master's servants.

Desperate to hide his sin of adultery, David devised a new scheme: *"In the morning David wrote a letter to Joab and sent it with Uriah. In it he wrote, 'Put Uriah in the front line where the fighting is fiercest. Then withdraw from him so he will be struck down and die'" (2 Samuel 11:14-15).* This time his strategy worked just as he planned. Uriah, David's valiant, devoted soldier was killed. After her time of mourning was complete, David took Bathsheba as his wife and she bore him a son.

Power corrupts good men! What a lesson we can all learn from this tragic story. Hidden within the heart of every man is the capacity to fall into sin. No matter how close we are to God or how elite our position is, we must stay humble and never think too highly of ourselves. *"Do nothing out of selfish ambition or vain conceit, but in humility consider others better than yourselves" (Philippians 2:3).* Like David, many a successful person has fallen into the insidious trap of thinking that they are above the law and better than the people they lead and serve.

David's weakness was the very one that afflicts many leaders in our churches today. He had a roving eye. His sexual appetite was not gratified by his own wives. Lusting after another man's wife, David stopped at nothing until he got what he wanted. Like King David, it has become a common occurrence for leaders to lust after other men, women or children. Tragically, the harm that they are causing to others doesn't deter them from following their fleshly passions.

It is obvious that the success and preeminence of these ecclesiastical leaders somehow empowers them to believe that they are above the law. Selfishness, fueled by the privileges of success, motivates their actions, where humility and concern for others once were their inspiration. Apparently, in some instances, their level of prominence diminishes their desire to control their passions. Like King David, deception and excuses take control of their thoughts, not the deep conviction and heartfelt honesty that once governed them.

The Curse of Sin

From the time of his terrible sin and the horrific cover-up, King David's life changed. Up until this time, everything he did was blessed by the hand of the Lord. His entire reign had been the envy of all the surrounding nations. No matter the size of the army that assembled against him, David defeated them. His power increased, as did the size and wealth of his kingdom. Beloved by his people, he knew the grandeur of one who is greatly beloved and honored by all. Popular, prosperous and powerful, King David lacked nothing. He reaped the blessing promised in God's word to those who walked in obedience to His laws. But now David was about to reap the opposite.

Sin also has its consequences. *"Cursed is the man who kills his neighbor secretly" (Deuteronomy 27:24).* David no longer walked under the beaming rays of God's blessing; but an ominous black cloud of the curse of his sin overshadowed his life.

Soon after David had Uriah killed, the Lord sent Nathan the prophet to King David. He told the king a story about a rich man who had many sheep and cattle, and a poor man who had only one ewe lamb. This little lamb was greatly beloved by the poor man. *"He raised it, and it grew up with him and his children. It shared his food, drank from his cup and even slept in his arms. It was like a daughter to him" (2 Samuel 12:3).* One day the rich man had a visitor. Instead of slaughtering one of his own sheep to prepare a meal for him, he took the ewe lamb that belonged to the poor man and prepared it for his guest.

When David heard this story, he burned with anger against the unjust action of the rich man. *"Then Nathan said to David, 'You are the man! This is what the Lord, the God of Israel, says, 'I have anointed you king over Israel, and I delivered you from the hand of Saul...I gave you the house of Israel and Judah. And if all this had been too little, I would have given you even more. Why did you despise the word of the Lord by doing what was evil in his eyes? You struck down Uriah the Hittite with the sword and took his wife to be your own... Now, therefore, the sword will never depart from your house, because you despised me and took the wife of Uriah the Hittite to be your own.'*

"This is what the Lord says: 'Out of your own household I am going to bring calamity against you. Before your very eyes I will take your wives and give them to one who is close to you, and he will lie with your wives in broad daylight. You did it in secret, but I will do this thing in broad daylight before all Israel' and *'the son born to you will die'"* (2 Samuel 12:7-12, 14).

David cried out in deep repentance. Mercifully, God spared his life, but the curse of his sin remained. Months later, the baby born to King David and Bathsheba became gravely ill. Despite David's remorse-filled prayers and seven days of fasting, the child died as Nathan foretold. This tragedy was just the beginning of a long list of catastrophic events that befell King David and his family.

The king's son Amnon raped his beautiful sister Tamar and, immediately after, his lust-filled passion for her turned into hatred. Rejected and desolate, she went to live with her brother Absalom. Two years later, still seething with hatred for his brother for raping his sister Tamar, Absalom took revenge and had Amnon killed.

Fearful for his life, Absalom fled to another land for three years. Scripture records that while he was in exile, David mourned for his son Amnon every day. As time passed and the sting of Amnon's death not so fresh, the king longed for his exiled son Absalom. After three years, David agreed to allow the banished young man to return to Israel but would not permit his son to see him. Two more years passed, and the king relented, revoked his decree to keep Absalom from his sight and embraced his son back into the family fold.

In the course of time, Absalom's true character was revealed. He launched a conspiracy against his father and attempted to usurp the throne from him. King David, leaving his ten concubines behind in Jerusalem to take care of the palace, escaped for his life. Eventually, Absalom and his followers overtook the palace. To show everyone his supremacy over his father, Absalom had a tent pitched *"on the roof, and he lay with his father's concubines in the sight of all Israel" (2 Samuel 16:22)* just as Nathan the prophet had prophesied would happen.

David mustered his men and a battle for the kingdom ensued in the forest of Ephraim. *"There the army of Israel was defeated by David's men, and the casualties that day were great—twenty thousand men" (2 Samuel 18:7).* While Absalom was riding his mule under the thick branch of a large oak tree, his long hair got tangled in the branches. As he hung mid-air from the tree, disobeying David's explicit orders to protect Absalom, the king's men killed his beloved son. King David won back his kingdom but his losses were too numerable to count.

The Missing Armor

Where did this beloved figure from the pages of Scripture go wrong? What can we learn from his mistakes that will keep us from falling into the same traps of pride and lust? It is recorded that just prior to his downfall, David made a disastrous mistake. *"In the spring, at the time when kings go off to war, David sent Joab out with the king's men and the whole Israelite army...But David remained in Jerusalem"(2 Samuel 11:1)*. Instead of being on the battlefield, David was strolling around on the rooftop of temptation. Bored, because in seasons past this had been a time when the excitement and the challenge of fighting the enemy had thrilled him, David now sought to replace that missing pleasure with fulfillment elsewhere.

Instead of covering himself in his armor, picking up his shield and wielding his sword, he was toying with the temptations of lust, the excitement of an illicit affair and the emotional frenzy of a massive cover-up. If David had his armor on, he would have finished the good fight of faith triumphantly. He would have avoided the curses that came upon him and his family and spared so many of his followers enormous amounts of undue suffering and devastating loss.

Perhaps, if we studied the lives of those tragic leaders that have fallen into the same snare of lust and pride as David did, we would see similar patterns evolve. Swords left to gather dust on mantles, belts of truth hanging on hooks of lies, breastplates of righteousness traded for worldly values, shoes that previously were ready to proclaim the gospel hidden under a bed of slumber, shields of faith standing in corners covered with the dirty laundry of justified sins. If each and everyone had read and obeyed the admonition of the Holy Spirit in Scripture, they could have risen as mighty conquers and not fallen to the position of defeated warriors who discarded their armor and compromised their values.

When the Holy Spirit intends to make a point, He often repeats the message. In this admonition from Paul's letter to the Ephesians, the advice is duplicated. Twice the Holy Spirit tells us to put on the full armor of God, so that we can stand firm against the attack the enemy launches against us. Then to make sure everyone fully understands just what that armor is, He goes on to explain each piece in detail. *"Finally, be strong in the Lord and in his mighty power. Put on the full armor of God so that you can take your stand against the devil's schemes....Therefore put on the full armor of God, so that when the day of evil comes, you may be able to stand your ground, and after you have done everything, to stand. Stand firm then, with the belt of truth buckled around your waist, with the breastplate of righteousness in place, and with your feet fitted with the readiness that comes from the gospel of peace. In addition to all this, take up the shield of faith, with which you can extinguish all the flaming arrows of the evil one. Take the helmet of salvation and the sword of the Spirit, which is the word of God. And pray in the Spirit on all occasions with all kinds of prayers and requests"* *(Ephesians 6:10-11, 13-18).*

If David had his armor in place, he would have been able to remain standing against the temptation the enemy commandeered against his soul. His kingdom would not have suffered and shame would not have etched his epitaph. The importance of this truth is undeniable. Embracing it will provide its recipients a safety net of survival. Ignoring it will inevitably bring catastrophic defeat.

Despite David's headlong fall into lust and murder, his humble character resurfaced. He never blamed anyone for the trials that came upon him—not even God. He took full responsibility for his actions, embracing an attitude of contrition. Once he repented, he never abandoned the God he fell in love with as a youth. Faithful in prayer, passionate in worship, devoted in his service to God's people; King David did not allow his terrible sin and resulting curses to bleed him of his dedication to his Lord. Accepting the discipline of his loving Father and the forgiveness He extended to him, inspired David to forgive himself and then all those who came against him.

"And we know that in all things God works for the good of those who love him, who have been called according to his

purpose" (Romans 8:28). What the enemy meant for harm, God turned around to benefit David. Out of the ashes of a ruined life, He brought forth the beauty of a life purified and one that was now completely dependent on Him.

"Leaders Suffer From Abuse, Too!"

"Obey your leaders and submit to their authority. They keep watch over you as men who must give an account. Obey them so that their work will be a joy, not a burden, for that would be of no advantage to you (Hebrews 13:17).

"Be completely humble and gentle, be patient, bearing with one another in love. Make every effort to keep the unity of the Spirit through the bond of peace" (Ephesians 4:2-3).

"..For out of the overflow of the heart the mouth speaks. The good man brings forth good things out of the good stored in him, and the evil man brings evil things out of the evil stored up in him. But I tell you that men will have to give account on the day of judgment for every careless word they have spoken" (Matthew 12:34-36).

"Everyone should be quick to listen, slow to speak and slow to become angry..." (James 1:19).

Chapter Eight

The Other Side of the Coin

In previous chapters, examples have been given of leaders like King David who experienced direct frontal assaults against their walk with God. So many unsuspecting victims faced frequent, calculated temptations from the enemy and fell far from God. This is not the only way that leaders are attacked, but just one of many. Even more destructive than those frontal skirmishes are the devious assaults that creep up undetected from the rear. It cannot be forgotten that the scheme of the enemy it to destroy the church established by Jesus Christ. If he can successfully take down the leaders, then the rest of the church is a piece of cake. In fact Scripture declares: *"Strike the shepherd, and the sheep will be scattered, and I will turn my hand against the little ones" (Zechariah 13:7).*

A dedicated pastor of a small rural church in the Southwest came up against a very problematic situation. One of his elders had taken a dislike to him. Something he said or did—he never knew which—had offended the gentleman. Sunday after Sunday the offense grew. Soon the idea surfaced in the elder's mind that he had the power to do something about the matter. Realizing that he was well known in the church and active in the community, he decided to use his influence to change the leadership of the church.

And so began the implementation of his scheme to rid the church of the pastor he had grown to dislike. Week after week, he visited members of the congregation spreading his slanderous reports. Those who listened were eventually bitten by the insidious bite of the same spirit of hatred that controlled the thoughts of the disgruntled elder. A plan was devised to withhold the tithes from the members of the congregation who were in agreement with the elder's stance against the pastor. They reasoned that once his income was depleted, he would have no choice but to find employment elsewhere.

A faithful member of the church heard of the plot to oust the pastor and informed him of what was happening. Deeply wounded by the report of the disloyalty of the members of his congregation, he resigned from his position as pastor. After leaving the pastorate amidst the assassination of his reputation and the attack against his finances, he was severely rejected and very disheartened. Alone, separated from those he cared for, he spent long hours in prayer seeking the face of God.

During these times of intimacy with the Lord, the Holy Spirit healed his heart and helped him to forgive the elder and all those who had partaken in the scheme against him. Realizing that he was not battling against a few men and women but against spiritual forces, brought the freedom and understanding he needed. *"For our struggle is not against flesh and blood, but against the rulers, against the authorities, against the powers of this dark world and against the spiritual forces of evil in the heavenly realms" (Ephesians 6:12).*

This revelation is one everyone must embrace to have the ability to quickly forgive those who have abused them. As this pastor found out by his own experience, one of the primary keys to forgiveness is separating those who abuse us from the deed and assigning blame to our true enemy. Recognizing that it is not Tom, Jane or a minister who has attacked us, but a demonic spirit that is using them, will help the healing process begin.

Abuse comes in many forms and does not discriminate against its victims. Leaders are the recipients of as much abuse as others within the church community. Frequently, it is the ministers of the gospel that suffer at the hands of those they care for and because of this abusive treatment, they give up the ministry. They are targeted by the enemy, because if he can remove leaders from the church, then an entire congregation can be taken out with just one blow. In this instance, not only did the pastor suffer but the church did as well. The powerful presence of God that the church was known for disappeared. Gradually, attendance slipped and the church became a shell of what it had been.

Manipulated By Men

When God calls a man or woman to serve as a pastor, He equips them with a heart for His people. They trade their own concerns for those of the men, women and children in their congregation. This gift must be mixed with wisdom or it can become an opening for the sly back door attack of the enemy.

A pastor's wife came to me with a familiar story. Her husband was devoted to God and deeply dedicated to his congregation. The people realized how soft his heart was towards them and began to take advantage of his good nature. Day and night their phone rang. Not with request for prayer, nor calls to ask for council, but appeals for help beyond the scope of a pastor: Would he go shopping for them as their car was low on fuel? Could the pastor's wife fix dinner for their family? A doctor's appointment was the following day and they needed him to give them a ride. On and on the requests continued to come with daily frequency. Consequentially, the tired pastor had no time for his relationship with the Lord or with his family.

These same families didn't tithe consistently nor did they keep any commitments they made to the church. When the pastor and his wife didn't comply with their wishes or run the programs in the church according to their liking, they threatened to leave the church. During this time the pastor and his wife contemplated closing the church and giving up the ministry. They had become fearful that their congregants would abandon their church, and felt like they were being held hostage to their unreasonable demands. The work load and the burden of caring for those attending their fellowship had become unbearable.

After humbly seeking Godly council, it was determined that he and his wife needed to get the Lord back in the driver's seat in their church—and in their lives. The Lord was once again placed back in His rightful position as head of the church. Decisions were made only after consulting the Holy Spirit in prayer. From that time forward their church flourished. Some of the demanding members left, but the Lord replaced them with His power and His presence. Once the Holy Spirit saw that no man occupied His throne there, He drew many humble, caring people into their healthy fellowship.

Sidelined By Discouragement

A newly appointed pastor of a small community church was delighted because the members of his church were growing in their faith and their dedication to the Lord. After a short time, the attendance doubled under his enthusiastic leadership. During the second year of his pastorate, a gregarious member of the close nit community began to attend the services. Asked by this new member to attend a local function, the pastor felt led to decline the invitation. Disenchanted by the pastor's refusal, the relatively new member of the church began to seek a reprisal against him. Angered and offended with the pastor, he began to malign the pure hearted pastor.

The slanderous rear door attack ensued. Because this new member had developed a close relationship with the other members of this fellowship, he was able to convince half of the congregants to leave the church. Overnight, the attendance diminished and the excitement that filled the once blooming congregation disappeared. This previously vibrant church floundered. For many months, the extremely discouraged pastor prayed about closing the doors and leaving the ministry for good. Feeling like a failure, he was convinced that someone else could do a far better job of growing and grooming this fellowship. Ready to hand the reigns over to another pastor, the Lord intervened. Just as he was about to give the keys to the church to another pastor, that man was given an assignment to pastor a church across town.

If the Lord had not intervened, he would have been sidelined by discouragement. The gossip and malicious back door attack against this pastor caused almost as much damage as the frontal assaults others have fallen prey to. I say—almost as much—because the story isn't over yet. This faithful pastor continued to seek the help of the Holy Spirit. Led by

God, he began an outreach program that brought hundreds of troubled teens to Christ.

Though the enemy tried to stop him and destroy his church, the Lord had other plans. Wearing the breastplate of righteousness, keeping his heart guarded by extending forgiveness and covered by frequent prayer, this pastor did not neglect the weapons of his warfare. Recognizing that he was not warring against flesh and blood, he took up the shield of faith and extinguished the fiery darts of fear. He began believing all that the Lord had promised him. Daily brandishing his sword, declaring those very promises, he soundly defeated discouragement. Today he humbly wears the shoes that keep him ready to proclaim the gospel of peace wherever the Holy Spirit leads him.

This pastor didn't just read the word, but he obeyed it: *"Finally, be strong in the Lord and in his mighty power. Put on the full armor of God so that you can take your stand against the devil's schemes" (Ephesians 6:10-11).*

The Double-edged Sword of the Enemy

Over lunch one sunny afternoon, a couple from a northern state expressed concerns for their pastor. They deeply admire this man and appreciated his tremendous gift of evangelism. Prior to their attending his church, there had been a church split. Deeply wounded by the loss of many wonderful people in his congregation, the upright pastor was transformed by this trial.

Fear gripped his heart and became an open door for the pastor to experience another method the enemy uses to demolish great ministries. Hurt, disappointed and suspicious, this gifted pastor became very exacting towards the unsuspecting members of his congregation. Fearful that another trusted elder would lead a revolt, he grew very controlling of all that took place in the church.

If members missed a mid-week or Sunday evening service, they were publically chastened during the sermon the following week. Furthermore, those who missed even one service were not allowed to hold a leadership position in the church. Every decision—even minor ones—had to pass by him for approval. Lists covered the doors and cupboards throughout the facility giving specific instructions as to how everything was to be done including where specific dishes and silverware were to be kept. Down to the smallest detail; everything had to meet with his approval before any change occurred. Fear now controlled the entire church. Those who felt called to leadership were held back by the unreasonable demands and unrelenting criticism of their pastor.

The sword that the enemy used against him had a double-edge to it. Beside the frontal attack of the church split, was the sneaky scheme of the enemy to ruin his future success by diminishing this pastors confidence, stealing his peace, and robbing him and his congregation of their freedom.

Once this couple understood the painful experience their pastor had undergone, they were able to commit to pray for his ministry. Furthermore, they understood that keeping Jesus on the throne was imperative in this situation. No matter what the reason, no man should allow another to exert inordinate control over his life. Jesus was given back His proper place in their lives. Staying or leaving this church no longer was the main issue. Instead, just being led by the Holy Spirit and knowing that His approval was all that mattered, became the new focus of their attention. They became confident that the Holy Spirit would guide them on their journey to serve Jesus exactly where He wanted them.

Guarded By Forgiveness

This situation reminded me of an incident that happened years ago. A wonderful pastor had come under a serious attack from many of the church leaders in his community. Slanderous, deceptive statements were being launched unprovoked against him and his growing congregation. The Lord sent me to this pastor with a word of caution.

I met with the pastor and explained that there was more to this attack than met the eye. The enemy's scheme was not just to defame the integrity and reputation of the pastor and his church; but he had another purpose in mind. Behind this terrible attack was a plan to engage the unsuspecting pastor into a place of spiritual weakness. I warned him to immediately forgive those who were slandering him and to call the church to pray for those leaders and their churches to be blessed. I encouraged him to resist the temptation to remonstrate over the injustices and to say only good things about the offending pastors.

That was exactly what he did; and the tables were turned on the plot to destroy this powerful ministry. Once he recognized who his true enemy was, he guarded himself with forgiveness. Covered by love, his back was no longer vulnerable to this sneaky back door assault. The enemy's attempts to engage this pastor and his church in hostility towards those who were slandering them failed. Prayer meetings were held and hearts were softened. Instead of division, a spirit of unity was birthed. Vision was imparted to this wounded pastor, and he began to assemble the local pastors—including those who were previously against him—together to pray for their community. Months later the pastor called together all of these leaders and presented them with a strategic plan to win souls. His vision for unity was accomplished when they all agreed to form an effective alliance to work together to bring the lost into the kingdom of God.

The Devil's Schemes

Most of the rear door attacks that come against ministers originate within the minds of men or women and proceed out of their mouths. Jesus warned the Pharisees, *"For out of the overflow of the heart the mouth speaks. The good man brings forth good things out of the good stored in him, and the evil man brings evil things out of the evil stored up in him. But I tell you that men will have to give account on the day of judgment for every careless word they have spoken"* (Matthew 12:34-36).

Jesus couldn't have been more straightforward. His warning against malicious thinking, and the subsequent speaking of those thoughts, was powerful, and one we should all adhere to consistently. Keeping a guard over our thoughts is the only way to remain safe from being used by the enemy to tear one another apart. Remember: *"but each one is tempted when, by his own evil desire, he is dragged away and enticed. Then, after desire has conceived, it gives birth to sin; and sin, when it is full-grown, gives birth to death"* (James 1:14-15). It is our own evil desires that originate in our flesh—or carnal nature—that become the open door for the enemy to tempt us into sin. Once those desires are toyed with and played through our minds over and over again, they then become the fuel that lights a fire of abusive actions.

Paul gave specific instructions concerning the guarding of our thoughts: *"Finally, brothers, whatever is true, whatever is noble, whatever is right, whatever is pure, whatever is lovely, whatever is admirable—if anything is excellent or praiseworthy—think about such things...And the God of peace will be with you"* (Philippians 4:8-9). Just imagine how wonderful our churches would be if we practiced what Paul preached. Instead of constantly finding fault with one another, our congregations would be full of loving people who are always looking for something great to think and say about one another. Praise would flow from our lips-not complaints and petty gossip.

Jesus taught us to treat others the way we want to be treated. None of us want others to look at us through a magnifying glass of criticism. To be treated with respect and understanding, having our strengths highlighted—not our weakness—is the way we would all desire to be seen.

Breaking old habits is not easy. But it would benefit everyone if we replaced our critical eye and judgmental thoughts with positive, praiseworthy ones. Following this directive from Scripture will help us eliminate these old worldly attitudes and formulate new Godly behaviors instead: *"Do not conform any longer to the pattern of this world, but be transformed by the renewing of your mind" (Romans 12:2).* Renewing our minds happens when we discipline ourselves to think according to the Word of God. Taking time to meditate on Scripture, instead of on the faults of others, will produce good fruit in our lives. On purpose and with solid determination, we must watch what we are thinking about and cast down those thoughts that offend God. Working with the Holy Spirit, we can gain victory over our thoughts. Instead of allowing every negative thought that flies through our minds to make its home there, we must embrace the resolve to kick those thoughts out as soon as they appear. Remember, fight to gain control over the thoughts in your mind; and you will gain control over your life as well. That is how bad habits are broken and new mindsets are formed.

The Tongue Has Great Power

The following powerful statement from Scripture, if meditated on and adhered to, could change lives and churches, too: *"The tongue has the power of life and death, and those who love it will eat its fruit" (Proverbs 18:21).* Satan and his army are quite aware that there is great power in our spoken words. If they can get us to speak words that will bring death, you can be well advised that they will make every effort to tempt us to speak against one another.

Paul admonished the church, *"A man reaps what he sows. The one who sows to please his sinful nature, from that nature will reap destruction; the one who sows to the Spirit will reap eternal life. Let us not become weary in doing good, for at the proper time we will reap a harvest if we do not give up" (Galatians 6:9).* It is clear that the Holy Spirit wants us to know that everything we sow we will reap. Good kind thoughts and words will produce a crop of the same back to us: words that bring life and healing. In the same way cruel, critical thoughts and words will bring forth a crop into our lives that we will not want to receive: words that deliver death, despair and discouragement. Rather we are instructed to: *"'Love your neighbor as yourself.' If you keep on biting and devouring each other, watch out or you will be destroyed by each other" (Galatians 5:14-15).* Living under the curse of unkind words we have spoken about others is not Jesus' plan for His bride. Living under the blessing and under the protective shield of the love we extend to one another is His desire.

Slander Devastates All

Gossiping, and consequently turning others against our leaders, is never acceptable to God.. *"Avoid godless chatter, because those who indulge in it will become more and more ungodly" (2 Timothy 2:16).* This too, will open us up to a similar attack against our reputation and relationships. If we sow discord and strife, we will reap the same. Once seeds are sown, they always produce a crop many times more prolific than what we originally planted. This is true when we curse our leaders with our unkind, disparaging remarks. *"Don't grumble against each other, brothers, or you will be judged" (James 5:9).*

It is never acceptable to slander another person or their ministry. Scripture makes it very clear: *"Brothers, do not slander one another" (James 4:11).* The end never justifies the means. Our method of handling injustice must be Godly: through prayer or directly confronting one another. Jesus taught His disciples the Father's way to handle disputes: *"If your brother sins against you, go and show him his fault. If he listens to you, you have won your brother over. But if he will not listen, take one or two others along, so that every matter may be established by the testimony of two or three witnesses. If he refuses to listen to them, tell it to the church, and if he refuses to listen even to the church, treat him as you would a pagan or a tax collector" (Matthew 18:15-17).*

Tearing down a minister's reputation to satisfy our hunger for revenge or justice is out of God's will. If we have a grievance with them, then they are the ones that must be approached—not our friends. Frequently, after taking the matter to the Lord in prayer, the entire issue loses its magnitude and understanding is imparted. If after a time of prayer, the issue remains troublesome, then a loving, honest confrontation with ones minister is necessary.

Loving Our Leaders

The Holy Spirit exhorts us, *"Obey your leaders and submit to their authority. They keep watch over you as men who must give an account. Obey them so that their work will be a joy, not a burden, for that would be of no advantage to you" (Hebrews 13:17).* In order for the Church to accomplish the work that the Lord intends it to do, we must follow His directives. Obedience to our pastors is essential if they are going to be able to administrate the church according to the leading of the Holy Spirit. We are exhorted to obey our leaders so their work will not be burdensome when their guidelines are according to Scripture and are not contrary to God's laws and teachings. Problems do arise when some ministers take the authority this passage in Scripture assigns to them too far. Their power to rule and govern the church should not infringe upon the rights of men or women to conduct their personal lives according to the leading of the Holy Spirit.

For example, some pastors feel that they have the right to expect those in their congregation to seek council from them about most of the personal decisions they are making: Should they change jobs? Whom should they marry? When and where should they buy a home? Where should they send their children to school? Once the leaders of a church become that involved in the personal lives of their members, the once caring community church takes on the characteristics of a controlling cult.

While in leadership training at a large church, we were instructed never to give advice to people who came to us seeking council for their private lives. Rather, we were taught to be wise and encourage these individuals to seek guidance from the Lord by going directly to Scripture themselves. This advice was sound. Inspiring them to develop their own intimate relationship with the Holy Spirit, proved to be very beneficial to all involved. It offered wisdom that protected those in the congregation against the abuse of authority by its leaders and helped the congregants to become more dependent on the Lord for their needs. This directive, most importantly, kept the leaders from taking over the place that only belongs to the Lord in people's lives. He wants to be their Lord, Savior, Master, Confidant, and King! Often people embrace the erroneous mindset that God will tell their pastors what He wants them to do. If this thought process is not corrected, leaders will be expected to act as prophetic gurus instead of the Godly caretakers God intended.

Respect for the God-given authority our pastors have over the church is never to be denied them, nor are we to ignore their needs. Withholding ones tithes to manipulate them or to destroy their ministry will generate terrible consequences. As we have seen in the example given above, those who deliberately succumbed to this practice often found that a spirit of poverty and manipulation was brought into their own lives. Those who continued to walk in unrepentance didn't reap the benefits of having their sins washed clean with His blood and having every curse broken. Reaping the effects of these unkind, malicious deeds proved to be very costly. Finding the church no longer filled with His presence, their income depleted, unpaid bills mounting, cars and equipment needing continuous repairs, or experiencing the power of another person's control over their lives: were just a few of the ways that these curses manifested against those who tried to control their leaders and destroy their work for Jesus. If they had recognized and admitted their sin to God in repentance, He would have cleansed them of their transgressions and placed every curse brought on them from their sins under His blood. His blood breaks every curse.

When things are done contrary to our opinion in the church, then that is when we must humbly obey the Lord and submit to the governing authority. *"Do everything without complaining or arguing" (Philippians 2:14).* Perhaps your ideas may be better but in God's eyes the best thing is to love. Loving our leaders by not indulging our personal preferences and is very pleasing to the Father. Praying with a heart of love for them to have wisdom in all they do is the best approach. Scripture exhorts, *"I urge, then, first of all, that requests, prayers, intercession and thanksgiving be made for everyone—for kings and all those in authority, that we may live peaceful and quiet lives in all godliness and holiness...I want men everywhere to lift up holy hands in prayer, without anger or disputing" (1 Timothy 2:1-2,8).* This approach is far better than trying to influence them to run programs in the church according to our specifications. Our leaders must answer to God for their decisions—not us.

Jesus established His church to be a place where everyone would be welcomed and loved. So much so that He said, *"A new command I give you: Love one another. As I have loved you, so you must love one another. By this all men will know that you are my disciples, if you love one another" (John 13:34-35).* That is to be our trademark. Love! We are commissioned by Jesus to display the same love that He displayed: a love that would cause us to lay our lives

down for one another. Let's start by laying down our judgmental negative thoughts and words about our leaders—or
our brothers and sisters. This first step will help us begin the
process of training ourselves to love as Jesus did.

"Learn
From the Past
But…
Don't Live in the Past!"

"Bear with each other and forgive whatever griev-ances you may have against one another. Forgive as the Lord forgave you. And over all these virtues put on love, which binds them all together in perfect unity" (Colossians 3:13-14).

"'For if you forgive men when they sin against you, your heavenly Father will also forgive you. But if you do not forgive men their sins, your Father will not forgive your sins'" (Matthew 6:14-15).

"'But I tell you: Love your enemies and pray for those who persecute you, that you may be sons of your Father in heaven" (Matthew 5:44-45).

Chapter Nine

Forgiveness: The Key to Recovery

It was apparent that Peter must have had some difficulties with his brother in the past when he asked Jesus this question: *"'Lord, how many times shall I forgive my brother when he sins against me? Up to seven times? Jesus answered, 'I tell you, not seven times, but seventy-seven times'"* (Matthew 18:21-22). No matter whom we are or who we associate with, people are going to sin against us. Jesus didn't tell Peter not to worry that his brother would never hurt him because his brother was one of His followers. No, He informed him that he probably would offend him many times. And each and every time Peter was expected to forgive his brother—if he wanted God to forgiven him when he sinned.

Often, when Jesus was trying to impress His disciples with an important truth, He reiterated it with illustrations. This teaching on forgiveness was so absolutely necessary for them to grasp that He told them a story about a king who forgave one of his servants an enormous debt. After that servant received the gracious gift of his canceled debt, he met one of his fellow servants who owed him a small debt. Instead of extending the same forgiveness that he had just received from the merciful king, he had the man thrown in prison until he could pay the entire debt. When the king found out what his servant had done, he called him back into his presence. Because he had not canceled his fellow servant's debt like the king had done for him, he told the man that he was to be turned over to the jailers to be tortured until his debt was paid. Jesus concluded the story with this impacting statement: *"'This is how my heavenly Father will treat each of you unless you forgive your brother from your heart'" (Matthew 18:35).*

There is much we can learn from this recorded encounter between Jesus and Peter. First, expect to be offended or sinned against by those close to you. If we harbor unrealistic expectations of one another, we will find it much harder to extend forgiveness. Instead, if we embrace a realistic appraisal of others, we will know that no one is perfect and all are subject to the same temptations. *"There is no difference, for all have sinned and fall short of the glory of God" (Romans 3:22-23).* If any one of us were perfect then we probably could hold others to a higher standard. But the truth is clear on this point. None of us are perfect; so we can't expect perfection from others.

One day a group of indignant men brought a woman who had been caught in the act of adultery to Jesus. The law required that they stone her. Wanting to trap Jesus, they asked Him what he had to say about it. Jesus ever so calmly, just bent down and started to write on the ground with His finger. Finally, He stood up and said, *"'If any one of you is without sin, let him be the first to throw a stone at her'"* (John 8:7). Many wonder what Jesus was writing on the ground. Could he have been listing the sins of those who stood accusing this woman? Perhaps. Whatever He did, each man, starting with the eldest, dropped his stone and left. Once the woman was alone with Jesus, He told her that He would not condemn her and asked her to leave her life of sin. This incident reemphasizes the truth that we all have sinned; and therefore, none of us should stand in judgment of others. Jesus was without sin; and He alone had the right to condemn this woman. But He didn't. If He who was without sin could extend forgiveness and mercy, then how much more should we who are sinful forgive one another?

The next thing we must realize from Peter's question about his brother is that we, too, will fall short of the glory. Just like the men who brought the woman caught in adultery to Jesus, we have sinned—and will continue to sin. A humble opinion of ourselves will keep us from falling into the same snare of pride these men fell into headlong. Though our sins might not be intentional, if we were truly honest with ourselves we would all admit to falling short on many occasions. Perhaps by a word, a thought, an action or the omission of a kind deed; we have disobeyed our God. A more truthful evaluation of our own lives would lower our expectations of others.

The third and most important lesson we must learn for our own good is to forgive. Just like Jesus taught in His story, this forgiveness is to be unconditional. No strings were attached to the servant who owed the king such a large debt. He forgave him freely; and He also forgave him immediately. He didn't put the servant in jail for a few days—let him suffer for a little while—but he forgave him right on the spot. He didn't weigh the amount of the debt and consider it too large to be forgiven. But the merciful king canceled the entire enormous debt. We are to do the same.

If we want to experience the freedom that true forgiveness brings, we must forgive just like Jesus taught us, too. Anything less brings bondage. Look at the lesson we receive from the terrible mistake the angry servant made by not forgiving his fellow-servant his debt. He was thrown in prison! Not only was he imprisoned but he was turned over to the jailers to be tortured. What happened to the unforgiving servant is a true picture of what unforgiveness does to us. It puts us in bondage where we are tormented by our resentful thoughts. Hatred and bitterness bind our emotions to the abusive injustice and hold us captive to it. Until we let go of the offense by truly forgiving our abuser from our heart, we will remain a hostage to the abuse we suffered in the past.

Hostage to the Past

Studies have revealed that victims who forgave those who had violently raped or attacked them recovered very quickly from the wounds of abuse. Emotionally they were able to resume normal relationships without distrust. They were not prohibited by the abusive event's effects from becoming active in their communities. But those who did not forgive were found to suffer the ill effects from the abuse for many years. Many of them experienced tremendous amounts of fear and some were never able to reintegrate back into the community. These studies affirm the necessity and the tremendous importance of forgiveness.

Unforgiveness always holds its victims hostage to the memories of the past. The injustice replays in their minds day and night. Without true forgiveness, there is no escape from these damaging, depressing images. In order to relieve the pain from the injury these memories bring, many gradually begin to consider acts of retaliation. Calculating ways to seek revenge against one's enemy is a very dangerous and extremely damaging activity. Furthermore, devising these retaliatory schemes can frequently lead those who engage in this pastime to perform actions that are as destructive— and in some cases even more damaging—than the original offense they suffered.

No matter what form the abuse takes or who commits the act, the ramifications of revisiting the events are the same.

True forgiveness is the only eraser that will wipe the slate of our minds. As Jesus said, forgiveness must be from our hearts in order to eliminate the constant replaying of the remembrance of the suffered injustice. Once sincere forgiveness has been extended, the results are dramatic. New uplifting thoughts are able to crowd out the old painful memories. A feeling of wholeness will begin to envelope one's life and hope starts to resurface again. The hope that life will begin to bring joy, and no longer just misery, returns.

Pray For Those Who Persecute You

Jesus gave us some powerful keys to be able to implement His command to forgive in the following Scripture: *"'But I tell you: Love your enemies and pray for those who persecute you, that you may be sons of your Father in heaven" (Matthew 5:44-45).* Deciding to forgive is the first and biggest step to begin the walk of forgiveness. Making a firm determination to obey God's mandate to freely forgive and love everyone all the time is essential. There can be no exceptions or any qualifications for those we deem to deserve our love or our forgiveness. In all cases and at all times, Jesus says we must forgive and in so doing love our enemies.

As we can see in the Scripture from Matthew above, the next thing Jesus exhorted us to do was to pray for those who have persecuted us. Once we take that step in obedience to His Word, in most cases the hostile, bitter feelings will quickly diminish in intensity. The Lord knows that this sacrificial prayer will activate a humble, loving heart in us towards our oppressors.

Not only that, but to pray for those who've wounded us to be blessed and prospered will reap a harvest of those same prayers back on our lives. We will always reap whatever we sow. In this case, instead of sowing curses towards those who have abused us and reaping the same curses back, if we obediently pray for our enemies to be blessed, we will reap those blessings we've freely extended. Praying for God to forgive those who have wounded us has great power in it.

This is exactly what Jesus did as He hung dying on the cross: *"Father, forgive them, for they do not know what they are doing" (Luke 23:34)*. This prayer purchased salvation for all that would believe and follow Jesus. We are freely forgiven and the curse of death is broken off our lives from the sins we've committed by His sacrificial prayer of forgiveness.

As we follow our Savior's example to pray for those who persecute us, we will inherit the fullness of His kingdom: *"But the fruit of the Spirit is love, joy, peace, patience, kindness, goodness, faithfulness, gentleness and self-control" (Galatians 5:22)*. His forgiveness bore abundant fruit not just for Him but for the entire world. The forgiveness of our Savior purchased eternal life for all who believed and many sons and daughters for His Father. *"The prayer of a righteous man is powerful and effective" (James 5:16)*.

173

The Power to Forgive: Found In His Word

After suffering a grave injustice, I was led to a passage in Scripture that reinforced my determination to forgive. Not only did it steady my resolve but it actually empowered me to forgive wholeheartedly. Many times we encounter abusive treatment that is extremely difficult to release to God with forgiveness. Knowing the truth that we are commanded to forgive, if we want to be forgiven, helps. But sometimes, it just isn't enough. This was where I found myself in the trial I was enduring.

No matter how I tried, I found I was being held hostage to the memory of past events. Though I offered prayers daily for the offenders, I still felt no long lasting release from the turmoil the abuse brought me. While I prayed, love flowed towards those who hurt me, but hours later the old feelings inadvertently resurfaced. Despite my efforts to forgive, the injustice replayed over and over again in my mind. Frequently, I found myself second guessing my actions: Could I have handled the situation differently? Should I have spoken up more vehemently? Maybe I could have halted the abuse by a different response? The questions persisted. The thoughts ensued. And through it all, I declared forgiveness daily. Determination to please my Lord motivated me to forgive fully and wholeheartedly.

Finally, the victory came. Gratefully, I was able to forgive from my heart by meditating on this Scripture: *"Do not repay anyone evil for evil. Be careful to do what is right in the eyes of everybody. If it is possible, as far as it depends on you, live at peace with everyone. Do not take revenge, my friends, but leave room for God's wrath, for it is written: 'It is mine to avenge, I will repay,' says the Lord. On the contrary: 'If your enemy is hungry, feed him; if he is thirsty, give him something to drink. In doing this you will heap burning coals on his head.' Do not be overcome by evil, but overcome evil with good" (Romans 12:17-21).*

Reading, meditating on and obeying His Word brought me the freedom that I longed to have. Forgiveness had been my friend; and I had experienced the treasures that it holds many times in the past. The trial that I was experiencing somehow caused me to find forgiveness elusive. After a season of struggling with my unforgiving thoughts, the release came when I experienced the power that is held within His Word. *"so is my word that goes out from my mouth: It will not return to me empty, but will accomplish what I desire and achieve the purpose for which I sent it" (Isaiah 55:11).*

The very power to activate what the Word is saying is held within those words. If we would apprehend the truth that His words are that powerful and that effective, we would find victory readily available in all matters—not just forgiveness. By meditating and believing—mixing faith with His Word—we will be changed from victims into victors. Jesus said it: *"'If you hold to my teaching, you are really my disci-*

ples. Then you will know the truth, and the truth will set you free'" (John 8:31-32). The truth did set me free.

Embrace Forgiveness

Like a trusted friend, embrace forgiveness. If you have been wounded by a minister, a church body or members of your congregation, in obedience to His teaching extend forgiveness from your heart. Freedom will be your reward. The multiplied wounds that visit your thoughts and scar your heart will lift and disappear. It will feel like an invisible hand has gently pulled them away. Healing will then be able to flow into your life.

Bitterness really does imprison us. It keeps us stuck in one place: fearful to reconnect with others; suspicious of leaders; distrustful of congregants; hiding away totally inconspicuous where we can't be hurt or used again. And just as refusing to grant forgiveness holds us hostage, extending unconditional forgiveness will set us free. Once you truly forgive, God's power will be readily available to release you to your destiny.

Imagine a little bird trapped in a cage and never allowed to fly. How frustrated that small bird appears, leaping from bar to bar trying to fly. That is how our lives feel when we are not achieving the purpose for which we were created. That little bird was made to soar, to fly freely unhindered. Nothing will make that tiny bird happy until it is released to fly. You, too, were made to soar with God. He did not make you to be imprisoned by sorrow or anger. He made you to take flight like a bird and become that man or woman of faith He created you to become. Once you release the forgiveness to those who wounded you, you will know that freedom to be all you can be with Him.

Let Him help you to become whole for many need the gifts He has poured out on you. Just like a wounded soldier cannot be sent to the battlefield; the Father can't send His children out to fight for those held in the grip of the enemy unless they are healthy. Bitterness, hatred and unresolved offenses leave deep, though invisible, wounds. They rob their occupants of their strength and their authority. In order to be completely healed and whole, the way of forgiveness must be followed.

Books are waiting to be written. Sermons, buried within the hearts of men and women, are longing to be preached. Souls, ripe for salvation, are awaiting invitations into His kingdom. Children hungry for spiritual guidance languish under worldly instruction. Those held in the grip of sickness are watching for the ministers of healing to come forth. The lonely and desperate wonder if those called by their Father will ever arrive to visit them. Jesus longs for your help: *"'The harvest is plentiful but the workers are few. Ask the Lord of the harvest, therefore, to send out workers into the harvest field'" (Matthew 9:37-38).*

"Wisdom Leads Her Children But Folly Deceives!"

"If any of you lacks wisdom, he should ask God, who gives generously to all without finding fault, and it will be given to him" (James 1:5).

"Since we live by the Spirit, let us keep in step with the Spirit" (Galatians 5:25).

"Now the overseer must be above reproach, the husband of but one wife, temperate, self-controlled, respectable, hospitable, able to teach, not given to drunkenness, not violent, not quarrelsome, not a lover of money. He must manage his own family well and see that his children obey him with proper respect. (If anyone does not know how to manage his own family, how can he take care of God's church?) He must not be e recent convert, or he may become conceited and fall under the same judgment as the devil. He must also have a good reputation with outsiders, so that he will not fall into disgrace and into the devil's trap" (1 Timothy 3:2-7).

Chapter Ten

Avoiding Abuse

M any throughout our nation are sensing that a new hour is upon us. Numerous changes have come into our world that are affecting every area of our lives: The financial markets on Wall Street, the banking industry and its lack of potency, the decline in the housing market, the value of the dollar, the political governing body of this nation, the lives of our young men and women and their families fighting wars in Iraq and Afghanistan, the security of the people in our nation under continual threats by terrorists, our sorely depleted education and healthcare systems. Along with every other segment of society, the church, too, has been dramatically impacted by these modifications in our world.

Dissatisfaction has overtaken the attitudes of the previously complacent populace within the borders of our nation. Adversely affected by the actions and decisions of those who held positions of influence and leadership, many remain skeptical. Leaders who had been trusted and embraced as honorable abused their authority and failed miserably. Some so badly, they were tried in a court of law and sentenced to prison. Fear etches the faces of those who keep abreast of the unfolding events echoed by the news media.

The church along with these other institutions has undergone the same in-depth scrutiny. Because the ecclesiastic leaders have been found wanting in their handling of the issues relevant to their ministries, they, too, are being looked at though suspicious eyes. The poor and disadvantaged have been ignored by many churches instead of being given the assistance that Christ advocated. For years laws that are contrary to Christian values have been enacted in our country without any objections from the leadership of church. Sexual abuse, hidden for years within the walls of the church, has come to light and continues unabated in many communities.

Scandals in all areas of morality have surfaced in the church: Pedophile pastors have been prosecuted for preying on youngsters within their fellowships. Exposed to public scrutiny, many ministers have been discovered being unfaithful to their longsuffering, humiliated wives. Revelations of the emotional abuse of family and church members by charismatic leaders has become commonplace. Frequently reported are stories of church funds that are mysteriously unaccounted for or stolen. Even more common are the accounts divulging the details of greedy religious officials who have lined their pockets with the money they have extorted from their sacrificing, sincere followers. Abuse and neglect have not escaped the church nor has the attitude of apprehension and criticism this behavior produces.

Paralyzed By Fear

People are being kept from actively participating in the local church by the fear that the stories they have heard recounted of abuse and neglect will surface in their church, too. Many I have spoken with have related stories of abuse. And interwoven in the details of their sad story is the revelation that these innocent observers learned a poor lesson. They learned to stay away from the church. Keeping their children far from potential pedophiles became vastly more important than seeking Godly instruction for them. Not allowing a pastor the right to dictate the course of their lives guided others far from church attendance. Knowing that their income might be sought after by greedy ministers, influenced many others to steer clear of seeking membership in a church.

Worse still is the fear that hinders those who have personally experienced abuse from the ministers of their church. No matter what form the abuse took, the effects are the same — avoidance. Those who have been under the control of harsh leaders avoid the church like a plague. To have been dominated and manipulated by guilt was worse in their estimation than experiencing the ill effects of a disease. Once free from that oppressive domination, nothing, in some of these victims, will permit them to open the doors of the church into their lives. Those who suffered from the physical and emotional abuse of a sexual predator wearing the cloak of the clergy, see a sexual deviant behind every ecclesiastical robe. It is no wonder that the church holds no attraction to them.

Many languish alone and without the support of close spiritual friends. The guidance of a spiritual father and kind overseer are not available to them or their families. Along with those benefits, the frequent, powerful prayers of sincere people are withheld from them because of the fear that blocks them from trusting others again.

Safety measures must be put in place and guidelines established so that these individuals can securely reconnect with the church and become actively engaged in it. Without the paralyzing affects of suspicion and fear, these folks could experience the benefit's a healthy church offers.

The Sad State of the Reconnected

Some have experienced the pain and disappointment of abusive leadership and eventually found their way back to attending a local church. Often these wounded individuals sit in the back of the church, arms folded across their chest observing every move the pastor and leaders make. Like a judge and jury they watch: Are there too many demands for offerings? Is the pastor a little too friendly, or is he too stand-offish? Do there appear to be too many rules and regulations giving a strong signal of excessive control? Does the way the service is conducted remind them-in any way-of the church they left? Are the church members friendly or fake? Is the worship sincere or staged? Or perhaps, does the pastor preach too long or too short a sermon?

Sound familiar? Those of us who have experienced the failure of a church body are probably thinking, 'How did you know?' It is the nature of all of us to avoid places that have brought us tremendous pain. When the courage and the desire to try again appear, along with it are the safety nets we have purposely attached. These safety devices establish an invisible wall that keeps possible abusers away. Though we are physically in attendance, our hearts are far from attaching to the fellowship. Suspicion and fear block the way until they are dealt with honestly and humbly.

Instead of manufacturing our own way of discerning if this place will be one that affords us the love, acceptance, and instruction that we need, we must apply the truths in the Word to guide our decision. Seeking wisdom from God is the safest way to know the truth. *"If any of you lacks wisdom, he should ask God, who gives generously to all without finding fault, and it will be given to him" (James 1:5).*

Parameters Put in Place Afford Protection

His Word, His guidance and His presence are the only safety nets we need. With His Spirit leading us, we will have the wisdom necessary to establish parameters in our lives that will keep us in control and balanced in our relationships. They will establish a much needed safety-zone and set healthy limits in our lives. These boundaries, once securely in place, will keep us safe-just like the walls of our homes do. If we are wise, we will make sure that the emotional edifice of protection we construct about our lives has a door in place—like the one our home does. This door will allow access to those good people that God wants to send our way. People, who will be there to encourage us, pray for us in hard times and help us enjoy times of refreshing and entertainment. God want us to be balanced-not lopsided in our walk through life. He desires us to spend time with Him, with our families, our friends and fellowshipping with our church family. *"Let us not give up meeting together, as some are in the habit of doing, but let us encourage one another—and all the more as you see the Day approaching" (Hebrews 10:25).* Being balanced is the key. Just like eating a balanced diet is the best way to stay healthy, so, too, keeping our lives balanced will keep our emotions strong as well. It has been my experience that this element when missing from sincere Christians' lives causes major problems.

Frequently, congregants pressured to spend inordinate amounts of time engaged in church activities, have gotten their relationships out of balance. Not recognizing that the level of the leader's expectations is too high and not attainable for everyone has precipitated much turmoil. Feeling guilty if they are not at every event or heavily involved in ministry, they have devoted an excessive amount of their time to these activities, while neglecting the other very important areas of their lives.

To avoid this pitfall, before individuals commit themselves to a church, they should establish parameters for themselves. This will free them from the pressure, or the temptation, to say yes to every request. Making mental notes or actually writing down a schedule, specifying how much time each week they will spend with: God in prayer, their families, at work, engaged in church events, and enjoyable recreational activities will help establish healthy boundaries. This is a powerful tool for implementing Godly wisdom and will offer the safety and security necessary to stay in control of their lives. Embracing this discipline of establishing boundaries will free each person to enjoy all the wonderful aspects of life that God has provided for them—without neglecting any, out of fear or out of the mismanagement of one's time. With their time being wisely managed they will live a better life—a life that remains connected with God.

The Safety Net of Wisdom

When I was a youngster, I learned a valuable lesson from my father. He was a carpenter by trade; and my mother found many opportunities to put his talent to good use. One of his projects was to turn the unfinished basement of our home into a large paneled recreation room. It was my delight to watch this patient man construct that room.

He began this project by using a strange technique. Taking a metal container that held a ball of string, he unwound a length of the line. Once it was extended, he covered the string in yellow chalk. Suspending the chalk covered line from the ceiling and attaching it tightly, directly to the floor below; he pulled the string forward and released it. This action made a long, straight, yellow mark on the cement basement wall. He explained to me that this was the plumb line. From this yellow chalk line he determined where to place the beams the walls would be nailed to. He told me that if he didn't use a plumb line the walls would be crooked. I watched as he used that line to guide him as he hammered the studs into the basement floor and walls. H explained that aligning the first stud with that straight line as his guideline, was essential for this room to be erected properly.

This principle in construction, which I learned from my father, has served me well. I have never built a building; but I have applied this truth to my spiritual walk. It became apparent to me that in life we need a plumb line, too.

Something by which we can gage the straightness of a philosophy, a teaching, or the character of a person by is necessary. It is just as necessary as a plumb line is to a carpenter. Through the years, I learned that God has given us His Word to be our plumb line. By His Word we are to judge the straightness or truthfulness of a matter. His plumb line will keep us from going off center in our judgments or getting off course. There is no short-cut to applying our plumb line. We must become just as well-informed in Scripture as a carpenter is of his tools. Reading the Word daily, spending time with the Holy Spirit—the Author of the Bible, and attending Bible studies are essential to knowing His Word.

Sitting under a reputable, trustworthy teacher is paramount. *"He must hold firmly to the trustworthy message as it has been taught, so that he can encourage others by sound doctrine and refute those who oppose it" (Titus 1:9).* Our leader should be knowledgeable of the Scriptures and able to communicate that information to us. Furthermore, the church we attend should believe in the totality of the Bible. It is essential that nothing be added to or taken from Scripture. Taking certain Scriptures out of context and interpreting them to manipulate people to do something the pastor wants, should never happen. This is an abuse of the Word and the authority of the minister. If you are educated in the Scriptures, it will be apparent when this happens. It is important for us all to know the truth so that we can refute false doctrine. Using the plumb line of the Word, one can easily recognize if a teaching is full of the opinion of the person teaching or just purely the unadulterated truth.

Hold Fast to the Word of God

We must hold fast to the Word of God. Ingesting the marvelous truths it contains will fill us with the wisdom we need for our lives. Reading His Word daily is invaluable. Communion with the Holy Spirit is not wasting time but is an essential ingredient needed to equip us for future endeavors. It will open our understanding and give us a wealth of wisdom concerning all matters. Some people read the Bible like it is a history book. If that becomes your approach, then you will be limiting the Holy Spirit. We must see the Bible for what it truly is—the revelation of Jesus Christ to the world. Reading it will position us to encounter the living Christ daily. His heart will be exposed for us to see. His desires will be made clear. But above all else, His magnanimous love for us will be revealed. God will show us who He is as we encounter Him in His Word.

We will see His great power as we read the accounts of creation. The simplicity with which He spoke and created everything out of nothing will inspire us. Just understanding His enormity will put all of our problems in prospective. For example: If He could speak a word and create the sun, moon and the stars, then He can speak a word over my circumstances and change them. Meditating on His enormous holiness as He revealed Himself to Abraham and to Moses will inspire us to trust the God who is perfect in all His ways. Knowing that the God who is infinitely holy dwells is us will engender confidence that we can become the righteousness of God in Christ Jesus. *"God made him who had no sin to be sin for us, so that in him we might become the righteousness of God" (2 Corinthians 5:21).*

Reading the accounts of the life of Christ in the New Testament will reveal (just to name a few): How great the Father's love for us is. The incredible love and obedience of Jesus for His Father that He would do only those things that He knew His Father wanted Him to do—even die on the cross for our sins. We will also learn about the great Gift that the Father bestowed on us by giving those who believe in and obey His Son the Holy Spirit to dwell in them. Reading about Jesus will inspire devotion to Him that no man can impart. As we meditate on the beginnings of the early church, the Holy Spirit will enlighten our minds and guide our steps into all truth. The plumb line of the instructions given to the church by the Holy Spirit, as it went through its birth pains and developed, will give us something to align our church next to.

There is no substitute for reading and studying the Scriptures yourself. God gave us His Word so that we could study and find ourselves approved. *"Do your best to present yourself to God as one approved, a workman who does not need to be ashamed and who correctly handles the word of truth" (2 Timothy 2:15)*. If we rely on others for our teaching and understanding of His Word, we can become easily deceived. Scripture warns: *"Do not be carried away by all kinds of strange teachings" (Hebrews 13:9)*. Without a plumb line in our own hands, how will we know if someone is teaching us the truth—or a slanted version of the truth? Many have been misled because they didn't take the time, or have the confidence, to read the Word themselves.

"Your word is a lamp to my feet and a light for my path" (Psalm 119:105. The light is placed on our feet to show us the way—not on our pastor's feet to guide us. Our pastors have to get their own light to guide themselves into all truth. We are all responsible to receive the light of God's guidance and instruction ourselves from His word. The pastor's sermons should serve as a frequent confirmation of what we have heard the Holy Spirit speak to us personally in our own private prayer times. These men and women are commissioned by God to watch over our souls—to equip us with an understanding of God's word so that we will not be deceived. *"They keep watch over you as one who must give an account" (Hebrews 13:17)*. Their instruction should help to fill out our knowledge of God and assist us to enliven our faith. But their teaching is not meant to be all we receive of the good healthy spiritual food our spirits require to sustain us. We must embrace the custom of nourishing ourselves daily with the Word, then we will become the mighty men and women of faith that God has called us to be.

Maintaining control of our time and talents is essential for us to advance to our destinies. Scripture declares that we were all created for a very specific purpose. *"For we are God's workmanship, created in Christ Jesus to do good works, which God prepared in advance for us to do" (Ephesians 2:10).* One day we will all have to give an account of what we did with the talents that God wonderfully bestowed on us. We cannot give God the excuse that others had control of our lives and wouldn't let us do what we knew we were supposed to execute. One of the fruits of the Spirit is to be self-controlled — not others controlled — nor are we to control another (see Galatians 5:22). It is imperative that we remain in control of our lives.

Another common deterrent to remember is: don't lose your life when you try to help others. If someone requires help: stop and help them, like the Good Samaritan did (see Luke 10:25-37). Then, continue on completing those things God has given you to accomplish. Often we get side tracked by the demands of others; and just as frequently, we become engrossed in the problems of those we encounter. Staying focused on the assignment God has placed on your heart will keep you in the driver's seat to your destiny.

Character Is the Father's Qualification

When we are looking for a church, if we adhere to a noteworthy instruction Jesus taught His disciples, it will help us discern where we should or should not go. *"Watch out for false prophets. They come to you in sheep's clothing, but inwardly they are ferocious wolves. By their fruit you will recognize them. Do people pick grapes from thorn bushes, or figs from thistle? Likewise every good tree bears good fruit, but a bad tree bears bad fruit. A good tree cannot bear bad fruit, and a bad tree cannot bear good fruit. Every tree that does not bear good fruit is cut down and thrown into the fire. Thus, by their fruit you will recognize them.*

"Not everyone who says to me, 'Lord, Lord' will enter the kingdom of heaven, but only he who does the will of my Father who is in heaven" (Matthew 7:15-21). In this Scripture, Jesus was talking specifically about ecclesiastic leaders or prophets. These prophets were men or women who spoke on behalf of God. They were given messages from God and were responsible to deliver them to the people. Jesus warned that many who appeared to know God and who pretended to speak his word and even preformed miracles were phony. These people may have had a powerful gifting but they lacked Godly character. Just having an ability to pray or proclaim God's word does not mean that person is trustworthy. Jesus warned that some of those very prophets were as dangerous as ferocious wolves. Very emphatically, He warned His friends to watch out for them. Just like a fierce wolf, they would tear them apart.

That warning was not just for His disciples two thousand years ago, but it was spoken for us today as well. Jesus advised that we examine the fruit of the lives of those who lead the ministry we are considering attending. Are the fruits of the Spirit evident in their lives: love, joy, peace, patience, kindness, goodness, faithfulness, gentleness, and self-control? Is the character of Jesus portrayed in their lives? Does consideration for the concerns of others take precedence over their own interests? Are they generous with the poor, sharing with those in need? When they are advocating a cause or a perhaps a building fund, are they harsh and demanding? Or does gentleness mark their actions and instructions? Does understanding undergird their decisions; or are their demands exacting and unreasonable?

In obedience to Scripture, it is important and for us to observe the lifestyle of the leadership before we apply for membership. *"Now the overseer must be above reproach, the husband of but one wife, temperate, self-controlled, respectable, hospitable, able to teach, not given to drunkenness, not violent, not quarrelsome, not a lover of money. He must manage his own family well and see that his children obey him with proper respect. (If anyone does not know how to manage his own family, how can he take care of God's church?) He must not be e recent convert, or he may become conceited and fall under the same judgment as the devil. He must also have a good reputation with outsiders, so that he will not fall into disgrace and into the devil's trap" (1 Timothy 3:2-7).* Does the pastor's life line up with the standards set forth in the Word of God? Are the leaders in the church talking like Christians but not putting their words into practice? When we are listening are they saying all the right things but behaving differently when they think that no one sees them? Are they living by a different standard than that which they set for their followers? Do they live lavish lifestyles expecting those who have little to sacrifice to support them?

Obedience to the Father is the measure by which God will judge the veracity of a person. That is the same measure we are admonished to use when we look for a fellowship. Do the governing officials of the church obey the rules of the township they reside in? Or do they consider themselves above the law? Are they faithful in paying their taxes and scrupulous about following the monetary regulations that govern churches? Do they adhere to the Ten Commandments or find excuses to ignore God's law as it applies to them? Are they faithful to their wives or husbands? Do they raise their children according to Biblical standards? These are just some of the questions that one should consider when making a decision to join a church.

Never forget, we must look for the character of Jesus to be reflected in the lives of those we allow to lead us and instruct our families. No man is perfect. Flaws will be apparent in everyone. But the standards that Jesus set forth must be followed, if we are to remain safe within a Christian fellowship.

I encourage you to let go of those guidelines birthed in fear that have held you hostage and paralyzed you from joining the church. A treasure of inspiration, the wealth of answered prayers, the excitement of newfound friendships, and the valuable gift of increased revelations awaits you as a member of the body of Christ.

"The Rich Treasure Of His Church!"

"and on this rock I will build my church, and the gates of Hades will not overcome it" (Matthew 16: 18).

"For the husband is the head of the wife as Christ is the head of the church, his body, of which he is the Savior. Now as the church submits to Christ..." (Ephesians 5:23-24).

"Just as each of us has one body with many members, and these members do not all have the same function, so in Christ we who are many form one body, and each member belongs to all the others. We have different gifts, according to the grace given to us" (Romans 12:4-6).

"Now you are the body of Christ, and each of you is a part of it. And in the church God has appointed first of all apostles, second prophets, third teachers, then workers of miracles, also those having gifts of healing, those able to help others, those with gifts of administration, and those speaking in different kinds of tongues" (1 Corinthians 12:27-28).

Chapter Eleven

Being a Part of God's Great Church

S cripture exhorts husbands to love their wives as Christ loves His church. What a statement that is! *"Husbands, love your wives, just as Christ loved the church and gave himself up for her to make her holy..." (Ephesians 5:25).* For God to compare the love of a dutiful husband for his beloved bride, to the love Jesus has for His church is astonishing and enlightening. Would a man allow a stranger to come into his home and harm his wife? Never! Would he permit anyone to destroy his beloved's reputation if he could help it? No! Then will Jesus just sit back and let the devil destroy His treasured bride? The answer can only be, no!

When Jesus was talking about His church, He declared, *"and the gates of Hades will not overcome it" (Matthew 16: 18).* His word is true. Whatever He says He most certainly will do. Satan and all his hosts will not defeat Christ's bride.

The purpose for which it was instituted will be realized. His bride will not be overcome—not even by the sly tricks of the enemy to drag the church into compromise and sin.

Nor will the body of Christ be ruined by the diabolical schemes to bring division. *"Every kingdom divided against itself will be ruined, and every city or household divided against itself will not stand" (Matthew 12:25).* If division can destroy, then unity must be reestablished for Jesus to implement His plan to raise up His church. *"I will signal for them and gather them in. Surely I will redeem them; they will be as numerous as before" (Zechariah 10:8).*

God's Army Will Prevail

Nations are only as strong as their military might. Those countries that have a well trained, powerful military are respected in the global community and never intimidated or manipulated by others weaker than themselves. The decrees and global regulations of the leaders of these influential nations are backed up by a force others feel is far too formidable to challenge. Maintaining a well-trained unified and heavily equipped army is essential to the well-being of the citizens of those dominant countries.

History has revealed that an army such as this can march together into battle and win great victories. World Wars I and II were won by the united efforts of not just one army but the consolidated efforts of unified nations. The incredible force of unity is astounding.

The church is an army. It is the spiritual army of God empowered by the Holy Spirit to fight the forces of evil: *"Finally, be strong in the Lord and in his mighty power. Put on the full armor of God so that you can take your stand against the devil's schemes. For our struggle is not against flesh and blood, but against the rulers, against the authorities, against the powers of this dark world and against the spiritual forces of evil in the heavenly realms" (Ephesians 6:10-12).* And just as a natural army can do great exploits, so too, the church can achieve powerful deeds as well—if it is unified! God's spiritual army must be well trained, heavily equipped and unified in order for it to be a formidable force against evil.

The night before Jesus was crucified He prayed for the unity of this spiritual army: *"My prayer is not for them alone. I pray also for those who will believe in me through their message that all of them may be one, Father, just as you are in me and I am in you. May they be brought to complete unity to let the world know that you sent me and have loved them even as you have loved me" (John 17:20-21, 23).* Jesus prayed for the essential characteristic of his church—love— to be displayed through unity. Without unity—a unity that is birthed in a love for God and for one another—Jesus knew that their work would fail. No one's prayer is as powerful and effective as the prayer of the Son of God. Faith tells me that what Jesus prayed for will happen. He decreed it. He made His will clear. He wants a powerful united church—one filled with love and compassion. And He will get just that!

Working Together In Unity, One Body

During a time of intimate fellowship with the Lord, the Holy Spirit spoke to me about the condition of the church. The lack of unity, currently dividing the church, was making it totally ineffective. But the unity that He plans to implement within His church will make it power-filled and successful.

While I was praying, as happens occasionally to me, I saw a vision. To explain: A vision is like watching a movie play in one's mind. The visions I see are clear and last for a few minutes or longer. During these spiritual encounters, a very strong presence of God covers me, much like a feeling of being bathed in love. As this vision unfolded, I observed a large group of very small people diligently serving the Lord. They were working in an enormous valley that had massive trees in it. Working silently, the people in this vision were not talking to one another but were independently doing their own thing. It appeared that nothing was getting accomplished though they were working very hard.

The Lord began to explain; *"There are many little ones that serve Me faithfully alone. But all alone they cannot accomplish what a great army can do. It is My will that they* would be one: That the hand would join the wrist and the wrist would connect with the forearm. Disconnected body parts are ineffective. This is a picture of My faithful bride. She wanders alone down the hills into the valleys and is surrounded by large obstacles that she cannot surmount alone.

"Gather My bride. It is the hour for her to be gathered together into a great army for the work I have for her to do will only be accomplished by a united force. All the suspicion and jealousy must be abolished if they are going to follow My call to be one.

"I am asking for a great show of solidarity. Forgiveness is the key for the establishing of My kingdom on the earth through My bride. Yes, there must be forgiveness for all of the injustices of the past. Wait on Me once you have forgiven all, and I will lead you to those I would have you join forces with. For I alone know the heart of man, and I will lead you where the connection will be established to a healthy strong ministry."

Then the Holy Spirit began to speak about His wandering sheep in a more specific way. "The time of testing the water is over. There will be no more sipping from this stream and finding it polluted; then running to another, only to find it a place of rancid waters, or mere bedrock and mud, and no refreshing waters at all. This is not an hour when My bride can afford the luxury of running to and fro from church to church.

"For the time is short, and there must be a joining together of those who are of the same heart and calling. Yes, the day and the hour is past where you could spend years getting to know one another and allowing the similarities to surface and bring about a strong bonding. There is much to be done and only a select few are ready for the task at hand. Others will join once the work has begun, but I cannot delay the work any longer waiting for those I have called to be made ready. Too many souls are lost daily as I wait for the called ones to be made holy. For many are called but few are chosen."

Using a common item to illustrate His point, He continued, *"Where can a tire go all by itself? It will just sit wherever it was placed until it is connected to a car or a vehicle suited for it. Then joined to that machine, it can travel many miles day and night. My bride must allow Me to reconnect her to My chosen vehicle suitable for her use; or she will remain as a lone tire sitting, not accomplishing her task in her life. Just be willing; let go of all suspicion; and I will do the work of connecting and joining those who are like-hearted. All counterfeits will be readily exposed and have no part of My work that I have assigned to My beloved bride.*

He concluded, *"The work of My bride is to seek and save the lost, to heal the brokenhearted, lift up the downtrodden, deliver the captives, and announce the acceptable year of the Lord. This cannot be done by one man, one ministry, or one church; but can be accomplished by one God living through His bride—united in love with one another."*

The Vision Explained

Because I have learned from previous encounters with the Holy Spirit that all of the elements in a vision are relevant, I began to ponder the details of this impacting vision. Recalling the enormous trees in the valley, I asked my Friend what these sturdy trees represented. As He explained the meaning of the trees, He also revealed the significance behind the rest of the events that occurred in the vision.

The Holy Spirit explained that the valley needed to be cleared of the trees in order for His kingdom to be established on the earth. The little people were His faithful ones who were completely ineffective because the job was too great for them to do alone. Because of the hurts and disappointments of the past, they did not trust each other. No one would give anyone a chance, so they could join forces to take down the trees of opposition.

Concerning my inquiry about the large trees, He explained that some of the trees were pride, fear, jealousy, discontent, worldliness, racism and prejudice. The tall trees represented all evil mindsets that separate us from Him and one another. These are the obstacles to His kingdom coming in all its fullness to the earth. The largest tree in the center of the valley was the tree of independence. This independence was fed by all the other trees: suspicion, envy, jealousy, fear, rebellion, hatred, a spirit of religion...

I thought of the great work that John the Baptist did to prepare mankind for the wonderful visitation from God. He told the people to get ready for Jesus' coming by preaching a message of repentance. Basically, he told them to get rid of all the sin in their lives or they would not recognize the Messiah when He appeared.

Sin separates us from God and one another. Getting rid of sin clears the way for people to receive Jesus in all His fullness. Those who listened and obeyed John's instructions to repent of their sins were blessed and became Jesus' followers and His friends. Their sins were no different than ours. And independence from God fueled them then, just like it does today. Humility topples the trees of self-righteousness, pride and hatred. Embracing an attitude of dependence on God and submission to His authority prepares the way for us to inherit the riches of His kingdom.

Trees Toppled and Angels Dispatched

Then I saw the vision again. Things were changing. Now I observed the little people begin to work together. Very quickly, and with much enjoyment and diligence, trees started getting cut down. *"Together they will be like mighty men trampling the muddy streets in battle. Because the Lord is with them, they will fight and overthrow the horsemen"* *(Zechariah 10:5)*.

Then He spoke a most encouraging word to my heart; *"I will bring My people together in this hour. No longer can they remain segregated. But the hour is upon us for My children to 'bury the hatchet' of past injustices and resentments. Now is the hour to join forces and work in unity for My kingdom's sake. I have given My angels their command to link like-spirited individuals together. And it shall be done; for My Spirit is determined that this is the hour for the rejoining of the body into one cohesive part. Yes and your joy will be made full in this solidarity of unity. For I am the glue that will hold you all together; and My love will make all that is different alike. This will be done, not by power or by might, but by My Spirit* (see Zechariah 4:6)."

Then I heard the cry of the Spirit; *"Clear the land, clear the land. For this is the day and the hour long spoken about by the prophets. Sound the trumpet in Zion. Assemble My people for the great day of the Lord is fast approaching. Assemble the troupes. Gather My army; My great end-time army. It is time to march together as one against the forces of darkness and rescue My children from the forces of evil. Assemble My army! Raise up My warriors!"* (See Joel 2.)

I knew I was hearing the Father command His angels to labor amongst us on the earth and gather His people into the great end-time army (see Zechariah 6: 5-8).

Vehemently, He declared; *"The hour is upon us for the great gathering of the end-time harvest, and it will be done in unity by My people. If I can assemble an army from a valley filled with dry bones; I can assemble an army from a gathering of disconnected people (see Ezekiel 37:1-14). I can and I will!! Watch and you will see My glory and My power manifest through this magnificent army. For it surely will be done - not by power or by might but by My Spirit.*

"You have heard My command. The hour is now; for My command has been given to My angels. They have been released to the earth as I speak and have begun the work. You will see the fruit of their labors as individuals join others in serving Me, and also as ministries join with one another to accomplish what they could not alone. Watch, for this great unifying work has started. It will be a quick work, My friend."

"'In that day each of you will invite his neighbor to sit under his vine and fig tree,' declares the Lord Almighty" *(Zechariah 3: 10).*

The Purpose of the Church

The church was established by Christ to do great exploits. Much more than just a gathering place for families, Jesus laid the foundation for the church to be a mighty force against evil. It was established to help mankind. God's plan is that this tremendous good will be accomplished by a skilled, elite force. To accomplish this God has appointed leaders to equip His army. *"It was he who gave some to be prophets, some to be evangelists, and some to be pastors and teachers, to prepare God's people for works of service, so that the body of Christ may be built up until we all reach unity in the faith and in the knowledge of the Son of God and become mature..." (Ephesians 4:11-13).*

The main purpose of the hierarchy of the church is to train and teach its members so they can effectively implement the victory Jesus championed on Calvary. *"All Scripture is God-breathed and is useful for teaching, rebuking, correcting and training in righteousness, so that the man of God may be thoroughly equipped for every good work" (2 Timothy 3:16).* Only those taught the Word and trained as mighty warriors in His army will be able to conquer the defeated foe—Satan and his demons. Using the weapons of their warfare, they can make the enemy release those they hold captive. It is the plan of God that everyone is to be equipped to fight for the souls of men. None are exempt or disqualified if they will submit to being trained by the leaders in His church.

As Paul directed Timothy and Titus two thousand years ago, he would tell ecclesiastic leaders today: *"You must teach what is in accord with sound doctrine. Teach the older men to be temperate, worthy of respect, self-controlled, and sound in faith, in love and in endurance" (Titus 2:1-2).* The Holy Spirit makes it very clear through Paul's instructions that it is the solemn responsibility of those who hold positions of leadership within the church to train and equip its members in righteousness. In Paul's letter to Titus he outlined many areas that needed to be addressed and fortified. Through his directives leaders are encouraged to teach the men to say "No" to ungodliness and worldly passions. The women were to be instructed to be reverent, not to be slanderers, nor to be heavy drinkers. He also taught them to remind the people to obey their rulers, to be kind and considerate and to show humility towards everyone. Great advice for leaders to use to raise up a church that will be a shining light in a dark world!

The army of Jesus Christ has the right and the duty to rescue the oppressed. It was given to them by Jesus when he told His church to use His authority to set the captives free. Before He left the earth to return to His Father, Jesus told His followers, *"'All authority in heaven and on earth has been given to me. Therefore go and make disciples of all nations'" (Matthew 28:18-19).* In other words: Satan previously ruled the earth and now Jesus does.

Three Changes in Authority

The authority to rule the earth has changed hands three times. After God created the earth He gave Adam and Eve the authority to govern it. *"God blessed them and said to them, 'Be fruitful and increase in number; fill the earth and subdue it. Rule over the fish of the sea and the birds of the air and over every living creature that moves on the ground'" (Genesis 1: 28).* Thus God gave Adam and Eve the free gift to rule over and subdue the earth. They were in charge of everything on the earth. God gave them only one directive. Don't eat the fruit from the tree of the knowledge of good and evil. It sounds pretty easy. They were the ruling king and queen of the earth. If they just followed God's one law they would live forever—happy, healthy, and very rich. But...

The second exchange of authority came about through a trick of the enemy on the first man and woman. Following Satan's devious suggestion to disobey the one directive that God had given them, Adam and Eve sinned and ate the forbidden fruit. Sin always brings death and separation. The consequences of their sin were grave. Inadvertently, Adam and Eve gave the authority God had given them to rule over the earth to Satan. When they disobeyed God, they lost everything. Eternal life was gone. They would not live forever but would know death. Sickness and diseases could attack them. Adam and Eve were ejected from their palatial garden and sent out into the world to work the ground by the sweat of their brow. Separated from all they knew and from the sweet fellowship they held with God, they lost their crowns and the keys to govern the earth.

The third exchange came in a very dramatic way. God sent His one and only Son into the world to pay the price for Adam and Eve's sins and for the sins of the entire human race. *"For God so loved the world that he gave his one and only Son, that whoever believes in him shall not perish but have eternal life. For God did not send his Son into the world to condemn the world, but to save the world through him"*

(John 3:16-17). Once Jesus died, was buried and rose from the dead, He turned the tables on Satan. He paid the full price for the sins of mankind and, at the same time, ripped the keys to the earth out of Satan's grasp. Now all authority in heaven and on earth was His. When Jesus rose from the dead He cemented His great victory over Satan. He's the reigning King and everything must submit to His rule.

As members of the body of Christ, our job is to administer His authority, much like policemen do when they enforce the law. The Father's desire is that we make Satan and his army submit to the authority of the new King, Jesus Christ. Once we are trained in using the weapons of our warfare, we can effectively make him obey. Any humble man, woman, or child can act as Christ's ambassador. Professing faith in Him and following His rule, qualify them to enter training in His army. These well trained individuals will be able to defend those trapped in the clutches of the enemy by using His name and wielding His sword, His Word.

Roles and Positions in His Army

While attending church, Christ's plan is that each one will be taught to effectively use the weapons of their warfare. *"Stand firm then, with the belt of truth buckled around your waist, with the breastplate of righteousness in place, and with your feet fitted with the readiness that comes from the gospel of peace. In addition to all this take up the shield of faith, with which you can extinguish all the flaming arrows of the evil one. Take the helmet of salvation and the sword of the Spirit, which is the word of God" (Ephesians 6:14-17).*

Just like soldiers in the military, those attending church have a major role to play in the outcome of each battle. If they submit to the training of their leaders, learn to use their weapons well and stand together in unity in battle, they will be victorious. Each and every piece of their armor must be in place. The Father's desire is that their pastors instruct them in standing firm in speaking the truth. Righteousness is to be held up as the standard for all to embrace. Because of their expert training, the members of His army will be ready in season and out of season to declare the word of God. Adept at using their own shield of faith, they won't have to run to their leaders for faith in a time of need. When the fiery darts of the enemy come against them or their loved ones, their shield will quickly extinguish them. Always relying on the grace of God and not their own efforts, faith and humility will anchor them to His presence. His thoughts will direct their actions. They will be adept at wielding the sword of God's word. Every promise will be held fast and declared against the enemy.

The role of the pastor is just as significant and even more challenging. His job is to get the members of his church battle ready—not to give in to the temptation to fight their battles for them. It is his responsibility to train and equip, not to win every war single handedly. He must be well versed in

Scripture so that he can impart that knowledge to his congregants. Always seeking the face of God and the direction of the Holy Spirit, a noteworthy pastor will get his orders from the General Himself, Jesus Christ!

When His mandate is followed and His army truly ready for war, resurrection power will be evident in every battle. Those held captive to sickness will be healed, the depressed and forlorn delivered, addicts set free, marriages restored, finances provided. As a member of an elite squad—the body of Christ—this is how the fabric of miracles will be produced: in the trenches of truth and unity.

His Vision for His Bride

God's vision for His church was enormous: First and foremost, nations could be reached with the saving power of the Jesus Christ. This vast spiritual army would defend the poor and oppressed, deliver those who are held captive by Satan's power, visit those in prisons, and heal the sick (see Mark 16:15-18). Through this mighty army much can be accomplished to benefit, not only its members, but the world as well—if it is trained and if it is one!

"Just as each of us has one body with many members, and these members do not all have the same function, so in Christ we who are many form one body, and each member belongs to all the others. We have different gifts, according to the grace given to us" (Romans 12:4-6). It is time for His

bride to assemble and become complete: The teacher joined to the preacher. The businessman united with the laborer. The visionary aligned with those who hear the still soft voice of the Holy Spirit. Yes, it is time for the hand to join the wrist and for the arm to connect with the shoulder. It is time for the foot to find its ankle and join the leg in running to accomplish great exploits in His name. *"And as I was prophesying, there was a noise, a rattling sound, and the bones came together, bone to bone" (Ezekiel 37:7).*

Through the unanimous efforts of the body of Christ, exploits of great magnitude will occur worldwide: Support for missionary work abundant. Villages destroyed by calamities rebuilt. The poor all over the world clothed and fed. Housing for orphans provided. Hospitals constructed and equipped. Alone we could never do all that God has asked us to do, but joined with others who share the same passion and vision, we can accomplish incredible undertakings. *"And let us consider how we may spur one another on toward love and good deeds. Let us not give up meeting together, as some are in the habit of doing, but let us encourage one another—and all the more as you see the Day approaching" (Hebrews 10:24-25).*

Reconciliation Will Bring His Glory!"

"But the wisdom that comes from heaven is first of all pure; then peace-loving, considerate, submissive, full of mercy and good fruit, impartial and sincere. Peacemakers who sow in peace raise a harvest of righteousness" (James 3:17-18).

"But while he was still a long way off, his father saw him and was filled with compassion for him; he ran to his son, threw his arms around him and kissed him...'For this son of mine was dead and is alive again; he was lost and is found.' So they began to celebrate... The older brother became angry and refused to go in" (Luke 15:20, 24, 28).

Chapter Twelve

The Riches of Reconciliation

One day Jesus was teaching a large crowd. Amongst the people assembled before Him were tax collectors and other notorious 'sinners'. Standing aloof and observing what Jesus was doing were some Pharisees and the teachers of the law. These leaders of the local synagogue were indignant that He would welcome these people and even eat a meal with them (see Luke 15).

Knowing their thoughts, Jesus began to teach His critics how God views His children by relating three parables. One was about a man who had a hundred sheep and lost one of them. Leaving the ninety-nine, he went to find the one that strayed away. After finding the little lost sheep, that man called his friends together to celebrate. Then Jesus said to those listening, *"I tell you that in the same way there will be more rejoicing in heaven over one sinner who repents than over ninety-nine righteous persons who do not need to repent" (Luke 15:7).*

The second parable concerned a woman who had ten silver coins and lost one of them. Immediately, this woman began to search diligently for that lost coin. Once she found it, she gathered her friends together and had a great party. Jesus explained, *"In the same way, I tell you, there is rejoicing in the presence of the angels of God over one sinner who repents" (Luke 15:10).*

This subject was so important, that Jesus told a third parable to make sure that everyone fully grasped the lesson He was teaching. And just like any great teacher, He saved the best for last. No other parable Jesus told exemplifies the heart of the Father towards his wayward children like The Parable of the Lost Son.

This story relates the condition of the hearts and lives of three people: a father and his two sons. Of course Jesus wasn't really talking about a father and his off-springs. These three characters represented God the Father, sinners, and the righteous. As this parable unfolds, Jesus introduces the kind-hearted father and then immediately shifts the focus from the father to his younger son.

This son was a wild one. He was sick of living on the farm and wanted to experience the pleasures of life in the fast lane. So he asked His benevolent father to give him his share of the estate. With no questions asked, the father divided his property between his two sons.

Soon after getting his inheritance, the younger son gathered together all his belongings and went off to a distant country. While in this remote land he sowed his wild oats. Not much time passed when the young man found he had squandered all of his wealth on his loose life-style. Poor, alone, and hungry, he hired himself out to a man who sent him out in his fields to feed his pigs. Starving, the younger son longed to fill his stomach with the food the pigs were eating; but no one offered him anything.

While working in the field, the hungry man began to think of his generous father. He remembered how well his father treated him and how great his dad fed his hired help, too. Hunger does that to you! It jars your memory and brings you to your senses. Suffering and being in want frequently causes the cloud of deception to lift and helps the rays of reality to shine through. This is exactly what happened in Jesus' story. This rebellious boy saw the light and decided to return home to his dad. Planning out his script, he knew just what he would say so that his father would accept him back. He would tell his father, *"'I am no longer worthy to be called your son; make me like one of your hired men'"* (Luke 15:19).

Jesus related that while he was still a long way off on his journey back, His wonderful, forgiving father saw him returning home. He knew this boy had had enough of his loose living and wanted to be restored. Filled with compassion, this dad ran to his son, hugged and kissed him. And he not only restored him back into the family but threw a great party to celebrate his return. *"But the father said to his servants, 'Quick! Bring the best robe and put it on him. Put a ring on his finger and sandals on his feet. Bring the fattened calf and kill it. Let's have a feast and celebrate. For this son of mine was dead and is alive again; he was lost and is found.' So they began to celebrate"* (Luke 15:22-24).

Here's where the parable takes a different direction and Jesus makes a very relevant point. He knew who his audience was; and there were more than just sinners sitting before Him. He had the indignant righteous there, too. Loving them and not wanting them to escape the full blessings their Father had for them, He directed the rest of the story to the Pharisees and teacher of the law.

Meanwhile, the older son returned from the field and when he came near the house he heard a report that deeply vexed him. His younger brother had come home and his father had welcomed him back with open arms. Not only had he been completely forgiven and restored; but his father was throwing a huge party to celebrate.

This older son was so angry that he refused to go to the banquet in honor of his brother. His dad went to him and pleaded with him to come inside and join the celebration. But the irate son argued, *"'Look! All these years I've been slaving for you and never disobeyed your orders. Yet you never gave me a young goat so I could celebrate with my friends. But when this son of yours who has squandered your property with prostitutes comes home, you kill the fattened calf for him!'"(Luke 15:29-30).*

The father made it clear by his actions and also by his response, that he wasn't treating the younger son any better than his older son. He loved them the same. They both had equal shares in his estate and both shared the love that was in his heart, too. *"'My son,' the father said, 'you are always with me, and everything I have is yours. But we had to celebrate and be glad, because this brother of yours was dead and is alive again; he was lost and is found.'"(Luke 15:31-32).*

Jesus didn't say what the older son decided to do. The story just ended there. Because the elder son represents the righteous, Jesus left it open-ended. He wanted those who are righteous in their own eyes to think about their own decision in relation to sinners. What would their response be? Would the Pharisees and teachers of the law see themselves and their critical judgmental attitude reflected in the older son's attitude? Jesus let the story speak for itself. He gave no stern lecture or any religious exhortation. It was up to them to decide if they would embrace the same attitude that the loving father displayed with his unconditional love and celebratory forgiveness. Would they embrace the repentant sinners and accept them into the family of God? Would they be willing to lay down all the resentments they harbored toward these wayward ones and call them brother?

The Sacrifice of Reconciliation

Because *"Jesus Christ is the same yesterday and today and forever" (Hebrews 13:8),* He is asking the same question to us today by the open-ended nature of this parable. Will you accept back into the family of God those who have left in disgrace? Will you celebrate with the Father when His sons and daughters turn from their sins and find their way back to Him? Will you celebrate their return or will you stand with your arms folded across your chest, stamping your feet in righteous indignation?

Will you declare, "It's not fair, Father. I have obeyed all your commands and served you faithfully for many years? I never left your courts and sought after the illicit pleasures of the world. I didn't steal from the poor, have an adulterous affair, or become addicted to drugs, alcohol or pornography. You never threw a celebration for me, Father. How come you are reinstating that fellow into your family, putting the best robe back on his shoulders, giving him prominence when he fell so far from grace? Father, why is he wearing the ring of covenant when he broke his covenant with you? Why is he being used to gather in the lost using your authority and your name? Why are his feet wearing the shoes of readiness to declare the Gospel to the world? Why him Father and not me?"

Haven't we secretly thought those very thoughts when we watch the Father promote those who sinned like the younger son? Jesus knows our thoughts and sees our hearts. He also understands human nature. That's why this parable so powerfully addresses the issue that faces the church today. How do we react when someone falls so far from grace? How are we supposed to treat a fallen soldier? Just like the Father did in the Parable of the Lost Son.

We are reminded by this story how to respond the way Jesus wants us to. What did the father do when the son left? Did he chase him, reprimand him, or curse him? No, he stood and watched. From his place of watching, he prayed for this delinquent son. That makes it pretty clear what God would have us do when someone we know or hear about falls far from God. Watch silently and prayerfully. Don't join the chorus of accusers and backbiters. Just wait and watch with a heart of love and compassion towards the offender.

Once the younger son truly repented, then we see a reaction from the father. Until the young man hated his condition and turned from it, the father did nothing. But once his son was on his way back, the father ran and met him. When we see our fellowman express true sorrow for their sins and turn from them then—like the father—we must run and embrace them. With our arm around their shoulder, we can support their efforts to rehabilitate their lives.

Repentance Is a Must

Let me be perfectly clear, I am not encouraging anyone to reconnect with those who have abused them. In the Parable of the Lost Son, Jesus taught that the young man truly repented, turned from his sins. His repentance was genuine. He even stated humbly that he was not worthy to be called his father's son but would become a hired hand instead. Then the father ran to him. Unless there is humble repentance, we are to do just what the father did. Forgive and wait for the person to return to us or to the church repenting of their actions. Then we can embrace them with a heart of reconciliation and acceptance.

As a member of the body of Christ, we must embrace the mindset of reconciliation Jesus taught in this parable. There have been occasions in the past when ministers have tragically fallen into areas of sin. In some instances, public scandals resulted. In other instances, we have experienced those failures ourselves from those governing our church. Some have repented, undergone extensive rehabilitation, and asked to be forgiven; while others have continued in their transgressions far from God and far from us.

God's desire is that all are saved and restored to His household. He always goes after the one. Jesus explained how His Father seeks after those who have left Him in the Parables of the Lost Sheep and the Lost Coin. The search is on. God is looking for His lost sons and daughters. He is determined to restore them, because that is who He is—a God of love and redemption.

When someone has sinned in the ministry—run off like the prodigal son into a life-style of sin—be ready for the Father to embrace them, restore covenant with them, and place the shoes of readiness to preach the Gospel back on their feet. Expect Him to clothe them in His righteousness and even throw a grand celebration for them.

The celebration could be revival. Are we going to respond like the elder son, with jealousy and resentment at the gracious mercy of our Father towards those who have mistreated Him or us? Instead let's embrace the same attitude of our Father; forgive fully and attend the revival party our God throws for them. They might be the guest of honor or the minister He chooses to use to facilitate the revival through. His ways are not our ways, nor are His thoughts the same as ours (see Isaiah 55:8).

He Did It Before and Could Do It Again

From the three parables Jesus told, His gave a very clear warning. Avoid becoming judgmental of those who have sinned. Do not react so harshly towards those who have fallen that you kill your faith in the Father's ability to change their lives. Resentment, coupled with unbelief, will produce stagnancy. From that insipid environment a mindset will evolve that will not expect God to restore or ever use these fallen ones.

But His message is clear; His grace is infinite. Even though none of us are deserving of it, He extends His unmerited favor to whomever He wishes. In His eyes all sins are deadly and deserving of eternal punishment. It is His grace that sets us free and allows us to be forgiven and restored. No one should take the stand that someone else's sin is graver than theirs' and therefore unqualified for His grace. This attitude could precede a tragic fall.

If we are not very careful, we could begin to question God's actions: How could God pour His Spirit out upon that person after all the things he did? They were drug users or alcoholics. They were dishonest in money matters. How could God choose them to spearhead a move of God? They fell into sexual immorality or were divorced and have remarried. We could miss a move of God—Spirit-filled parties like the elder son rejected—and determine erroneously, that this revival is not of God because of the past sins of those leading it.

Remember, God's mercy was large enough to embrace Peter and Paul. Remarkably, God called Peter to take care of His church, even after he publicly denied knowing Jesus (see John 21:15-17). The night before He was crucified, right after Jesus was arrested; Peter denied knowing Him three separate times. Each time he was accused of being one of Jesus'followers, he vehemently denied it. Fear griped the man who had been one of Jesus closest friends during His three years of public ministry. Yet, the one who failed Jesus in His darkest hour, was the very one He chose to lead the greatest revival ever.

Peter met God's qualifications. Immediately after he disowned Jesus, Scripture reports that Peter *"went outside and wept bitterly" (Luke 22:62)*. He had a repentant heart that was full of love for his Master. When the Father looked at Peter, He didn't see a coward or a disloyal friend. No! He saw a man whose heart was filled with love for Jesus—the love that covers a multitude of sins.

Paul, too, one of the worse persecutors of the Christian community, was called and chosen by God. Soon after the Holy Spirit fell on the disciples at Pentecost, a great persecution broke out against the early church. One of the chief Pharisees who led the tyranny against the Christians was Saul of Tarsus (later called Paul). Some died and many suffered and were tortured with his approval. While on his way to Damascus to imprison any believers he found there, he had a dramatic encounter with Jesus: *"..suddenly a light from heaven flashed around him. He fell to the ground and heard a voice say to him, 'Saul, Saul, why do you persecute me?'"(Acts 9:3-4)*.

This experience forever changed Saul. Once he realized that this move of God was genuine and that Jesus was the long awaited Messiah, he repented. The man who hated and tyrannized the Christian church became an extraordinary apostle and tireless missionary.

After his encounter with Jesus on the road to Damascus, Paul spearheaded a revival to the entire Gentile world. He, like Peter, met the Master's standards. That is why no man can judge the heart or the motives of another. Paul, to all who observed him, looked like a man who was filled with hatred. But the Father knew that love for God and devotion to His law were the forces that motivated this conscientious zealot. Once Paul saw the light and knew the truth, he did a one hundred and eighty degree turn around. He became a man possessed with a passionate desire to lead all men to a saving knowledge of Jesus Christ.

When the Father looked into these sinner's hearts, He saw that love that covers a multitude of sins. No man can judge what lies within the heart of any man. Only God can see the true condition of each person's heart.

May He find that same love that He found in the heart of Paul and in the heart of Peter in your heart. *"Above all, love each other deeply, because love covers over a multitude of sins" (1 Peter 4:8).*

For further information, you can contact the author at:

His Heart Ministries International
P.O. Box 5042
Salt Springs, Florida 32134

Or e-mail her at
hisheartinternational@yahoo.com

Donna's first book has inspired many and may be ordered by writing or e-mailing her.
The Mysteries of Heaven and Hell Revealed
is a stirring account of the author's impacting visits to heaven and hell.

Visit Donna's website:
www.hisheartministry.org

CPSIA information can be obtained
at www.ICGtesting.com
Printed in the USA
LVHW112247300721
693981LV00001B/6